THE
SCEPTICAL
INVESTOR

JOHN STEPEK has been writing about business, economics and investment for more than 20 years.

He is the executive editor of *MoneyWeek*, Britain's bestselling weekly investment magazine. Since 2005, he has been the main author on its investment newsletter, *Money Morning*, which goes out by email to more than 85,000 readers each day. *MoneyWeek* is well known for its contrarian investment views – most notably for warning repeatedly, well before the fall of Northern Rock or Lehman Brothers, that the collapse in US house prices in 2006 would mutate into a much more damaging financial crisis.

Before he became a journalist, Stepek worked for his family's business, a chain of electrical retail shops in the east end of Glasgow, but then decided that he would rather write for a living. He started out by writing articles about the specific business challenges facing family firms and now writes about all aspects of financial markets, from bonds to gold to derivatives. He studied psychology at university and has always been fascinated by the gap between the way the market works in theory and the way it works in practice, and by how our deep-rooted instincts work against our best interests as investors.

His work has been published in *The Spectator* and *The Sunday Times* as well as a wide range of specialist financial magazines. He has appeared as an expert commentator on BBC Radio 4's *Today* programme, BBC Radio Scotland, *Newsnight*, *Daily Politics* and Bloomberg. You can follow him on Twitter at @John_Stepek.

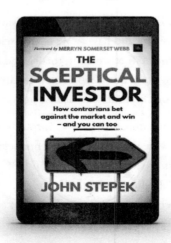

THE
SCEPTICAL
INVESTOR

How contrarians bet against the market and win – and you can too

JOHN STEPEK

Foreword by **MERRYN SOMERSET WEBB**

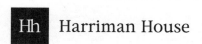

Harriman House

HARRIMAN HOUSE LTD
18 College Street
Petersfield
Hampshire
GU31 4AD
GREAT BRITAIN
Tel: +44 (0)1730 233870

Email: enquiries@harriman-house.com
Website: www.harriman-house.com

First published in Great Britain in 2019.
Copyright © John Stepek

The right of John Stepek to be identified as the author has been asserted in accordance
with the Copyright, Design and Patents Act 1988.

Paperback ISBN: 978-0-85719-627-9
eBook ISBN: 978-0-85719-628-6

British Library Cataloguing in Publication Data
A CIP catalogue record for this book can be obtained from the British Library.

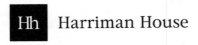

Contents

FOREWORD
by Merryn Somerset Webb

S TOCK MARKET INVESTING should be easy. Buy shares
when they look cheap. Sell them when they look expensive.
Repeat. Retire rich.

Easy.

However, simple as this sounds, it turns out to be remarkably
difficult to get the hang of. Almost all professional fund managers
eventually fail to do what they are paid to do – outperform the
market as a whole, after expense and fees are taken into account.
Most amateurs fail too.

That's not for want of experts offering advice. The first book
really claiming to be able to help investors find a path through
the markets was published in 1761[1] and there have been many
thousands since, all promising one way or another to let you
into the secrets of the mysteries of successful investing. A tiny
selection of titles: *The Theory of Stock Market Speculation* (1874),
Men and Mysteries of Wall Street (1870), *The Art of Money Making*
(1872), *The Game in Wall Street and How to Play it Successfully*
(1898), *The Art of Wise Investing* (1904), *How Money is Made in*

1   *Every Man His Own Broker; or, A Guide to Exchange Alley* by
Thomas Mortimer.

Security Investments or A Fortune at 55 (1906), *Psychology of the Stock Market* (1912) and *The Money Game* (1968).[2]

You'll note some common themes. Investing is approached as something that is unusually un-straightforward. There is a genre of books that suggest it can be simplified and categorised so that everyone can have a go, but the overwhelming feeling you will be left with after a flick through 300 years of investment writing history is that getting involved is very much a specialist activity. It is, as academic Nicky Marsh, a professor at the University of Southampton notes, regularly presented as being incredibly difficult to get a grip on (it is variously referred to as volatile, fickle, unfathomable, capricious, impulsive).

Attempting to manage it – even as a sideline – is also presented as highly skilled and mildly exhilarating work. The "true stock operator", said Thomas Lawson, writing in his *Frenzied Finance* in 1905, "is sometimes tempted to buckle on his armour and get into an exciting fight solely for the combat's sake and then he might not be over concerned about the rights and wrongs of the contention." The theme is picked up by 1990s guru Burton G. Malkiel, in his still bestselling *A Random Walk Down Wall Street* (1973). Most of the book is about how you can't beat the market. But the final few paragraphs of the last chapter reveal a little more about just how Malkiel really feels about investing. "Investing is a bit like lovemaking. Ultimately it really is an art requiring a certain talent and the presence of a mysterious force called luck... The game of investing is like lovemaking in another important respect too. It's much too much fun to give up."

2   For more titles and more on all of these books, visit the Library of Mistakes in Edinburgh.

The point here is that the history of these kinds of books tends to make investing into something of a super-exciting hobby, albeit one that comes with the happy possibility that you could win along the way (and make a fortune). They also offer a remarkable number of methods with which to manage your hobby. You can try and manhandle the fickleness of the whole thing into series of charts. You can try momentum – and simply go with the directional flow of the market. You can be a growth investor – chucking aside the stolidity of the past for the glamour of the future. Or you can be a value investor – using one of a hundred-odd different methods to try to transform something that is, by definition, a relative judgement into something absolute. Either way, or so the stories go, this just isn't for everyone.

This was all fine even a couple of decades ago. Until relatively recently most people could manage perfectly well without paying any attention to stock markets and their excitable commentators at all. Pensions were managed by companies – you worked and at the end of your working life the company paid you out a percentage of your salary, inflation-linked, forever. You could save anything else in cash and feel OK about it too. Until the great financial crisis of 2007–08 you could at least have relied on getting a return over inflation of 1–2% on your cash (against 5–6% for equities) had you bothered to keep even the vaguest eye on the rates being offered by deposit-taking institutions. Not great, but at least a positive result.

No more: today interest rates are very significantly lower than the rate of inflation and look likely to stay that way for many years to come. Every day you hold your savings in cash is a day during which you are losing money in real terms. The idea of saving is to put away money, watch it compound as interest is paid, and to then be able to buy more with it in the future than you can today. That doesn't work anymore. The pensions I mention above barely exist anymore either (unless you work in the public sector). Instead, in the UK as in most other countries, everyone is one way or another becoming responsible for either keeping an eye on or creating a portfolio of investments that will finance their retirements.

All this represents enormous change. It means that investing can't just be a niche activity or a hobby for other people. It has to be something that everyone is at least a little engaged with: at the very least, anyone who wants to get anywhere near a fortune at 55 needs to know how to pick and to judge fund managers.

This all requires a new kind of book – and *The Sceptical Investor* is that book. There's no mystery, no game, no art (and, I'm afraid, no lovemaking) inside these pages. There is also the bare minimum of jargon or complication. What you get instead is more than 15 years of experience distilled into 280-odd pages. The key message is the one the title suggests. Don't be rigidly attached to any one idea or one method. Just be sceptical and careful. That doesn't mean being relentlessly pessimistic and it doesn't mean always doing the exact opposite to what everyone else is doing (sometimes the crowd is right). It does mean noting that there are useful measures of value you can use to decide what to buy and when; that some fund managers are significantly better than others; that the next big thing is mostly less big than you think – but sometimes much bigger than you could ever imagine; that honesty and true transparency are rare in financial markets; and, crucially, that the cost of investing can be as important as the performance of the investor.

John has been writing about investing, and meeting with the key characters in the investment world, for over 15 years. You'll want to read what he has to say very carefully – and make sure that anyone managing your money reads it too.

MERRYN SOMERSET WEBB

Edinburgh, 2019

CHAPTER

1

What is Contrarian Investing?

Why every fund manager says they are a contrarian

I'VE BEEN WRITING about investment for 15 years. In that time, I've never met a fund manager who wasn't a contrarian.

No wonder. Successful contrarians are the closest things that financial markets get to heroes. A contrarian trade that pays off won't just make you a profit – it could make your reputation. Jesse Livermore, the subject of investment classic *Reminiscences of a Stock Operator*, became history's most famous trader because he made his (second) multi-million dollar fortune by shorting the market ahead of the 1929 stock market crash. One of the trades that made Sir John Templeton's name was his decision to bet big on beaten-down US stocks just as the second world war was getting underway, quadrupling his original stake in just four years. More recently, the hedge fund managers who made millions by betting against the US subprime mortgage market ahead of the 2008 financial crisis, had a bestselling book – *The Big Short* by Michael Lewis – written about them, which was then turned into a Hollywood film.

Big bold bets. Getting it right when everyone else gets it wrong. Getting rich while also being able to say 'I told you so'. It's very appealing.

So obviously, if a journalist asks you, as a professional investor, 'Are you a contrarian?', the only answer you're ever going to give is 'Yes'. Nobody wants to invest with someone who claims to blindly follow the crowd (even though that, in fact, is what a great many fund managers do, for reasons we'll explore later).

What do contrarian investors actually do?

Everyone knows a contrarian trade when they see one. Yet pinning contrarianism down to specifics is surprisingly hard. Most other investing styles are well defined. Value investors buy cheap stocks. Momentum investors buy stuff that has already gone up. Growth investors buy pricey-looking stocks that are growing quickly. Small-cap funds buy, well, small caps. You can buy funds with these descriptions in the title and you'll have a good idea of what strategy they plan to follow.

But what do 'contrarian' investors do? There's a vague understanding that contrarian investors bet against the market. They "buy when there's blood on the streets". They "zig when the market is zagging". They "buy what everyone else hates". These old clichés are right in certain ways – contrarians do all of these things. But the clichés are wrong in a very specific and harmful way. Putting the focus on what 'the market' is doing, suggests that the most important factor in contrarian thinking is to spend most of your time second-guessing the market.

This is profoundly wrong – and this misconception goes a long way to explaining why many would-be contrarians lose money.

Why I prefer scepticism to contrarianism

The basic problem with doing the opposite of what the market is doing, is that sometimes – often, even – the market gets things right. And even when it's wrong, it can stay wrong for longer than you can stay solvent (to paraphrase the great economist John Maynard Keynes, who learned this lesson the hard way). Some indicators of market sentiment can certainly highlight potentially profitable hunting grounds (we'll look at those later on) but spotting moments of 'irrational exuberance' or points of 'maximum pessimism' is only a small part of what a successful contrarian does.

And not all contrarians use the same methods. Some buy value stocks and hang on patiently for the share price to recover. Others make big, timely bets against investment bubbles, or simply avoid getting sucked into them. Others look for reliably cyclical sectors – buying on the downturns and selling when the good times roll around again. And contrarians understand that things change. The market arbitrages success away – the strategies that worked yesterday may not work tomorrow. In short, contrarian investing is a mindset rather than a specific strategy, which is why it's so hard to pin down.

This is why I prefer to think of contrarianism as **sceptical investing**. In fact, that's the term I'm going to use for the rest of this book. Sceptical investors do not define themselves in opposition to the crowd. Yes, they understand that markets make mistakes – a market is made up of human beings, and human beings tend to overreact in predictable ways. However, what matters is the scale of the mistake – the size of the gap between the underlying 'reality' and the market's perception of that reality.

The importance of perception versus reality

Investment author and strategist Michael Mauboussin draws a good analogy. Imagine a horse race. As a punter, you can look at the horse's diet, the form, the jockey – the 'fundamentals'. Those can give you a good idea of what the horse is 'worth' – what its chances of winning the race are. But if you want to make money consistently, this isn't all you need to know. You need to know what odds the bookies are placing on the horse actually winning. You won't get anywhere fast by betting on the favourite every time, even if it is the best horse in the race – the odds on offer for a winning bet won't compensate for your inevitable losses.

Sceptical investors make their money when the bookie is mispricing the horse's chances. In other words, where the market gets the odds wrong. So as Mauboussin puts it, it's not just about sentiment – it's about "how that sentiment can lead to disconnects between fundamentals and expectations."

So sceptical investors are always questioning assumptions – both the market's and their own. They don't take anything for granted. They do the work required to have as clear an understanding of reality as possible, rather than just working off a hunch or a nebulous sentiment indicator of some sort. This enables them to identify when markets are overreacting to the point where the reward on offer for betting on the gap closing between market perception and reality more than justifies the risk of being wrong.

If this was easy, everybody would be doing it

That sounds simple. In practice, of course, it's very difficult. If it wasn't, everybody would be doing it. But it's not impossible. And with the right tool kit and mindset – which I hope to show you in this book – you can learn how to be a more sceptical investor.

It is partly about doing your research. If a company's share price falls by 50% after a profit warning, you can't just assume the market is overreacting – you need to build a solid case for investing, which means looking at accounts and thinking deeply about which scenarios may unfold. But at a more conceptual level, it's also about approaching the market with the correct mental models (in other words, having a sound grasp of what really drives the market, rather than what drives it in theory), and having enough self-knowledge and humility to avoid being hamstrung by your own behavioural flaws.

That's what this book is about. In the chapters that follow, we'll look at how the market really works, and why the sceptical approach is a better way to look at investing, regardless of how active or passive you want to be. Then we'll move on to the psychology of markets, and how to think critically in order to take advantage of their tendency to overreact, while developing techniques aimed at restraining your own self-destructive instincts. Finally, we'll look at some of the most successful methods used by contrarians and sceptical investors today.

Let's get started.

CHAPTER

2

Why Sceptical Investing Works

T HE PREVAILING VIEW of markets – the dominant 'mental model' – is that they are efficient. There is a very long and technical explanation of the efficient market hypothesis (EMH) – indeed, I could write a whole book about it and barely scratch the surface or cover all the arguments and different interpretations – but, put very simply, the EMH argues that markets 'price in' all available data promptly, as a result of a mass of investors responding to new information as it arrives. That doesn't mean that prices are necessarily always 'right' as such (no one can predict the future), but in effect they might as well be. Beating an efficient market consistently over time should be impossible, because there is no way to secure a lasting edge over the long run. It also suggests that it should be hard or impossible for apparently obvious or predictable anomalies – such as massive, irrational valuation bubbles – to exist, or to survive for long if they do.

Confessions of an inefficient investor

Now, most of us would argue that this clearly isn't true, and to be fair, few but the most fundamentalist academics would argue that the market is perfectly efficient. There are plenty of examples in history of markets getting it badly wrong (look at the fallout from any bubble and bust of your choice), even when all of the relevant information is seemingly widely available. For example, during the tech bubble of the late 1990s, a CEO could put a rocket under the share price of their company simply by appending '.com' to the company name – no change of strategy or connection to the tech industry required.

And if you're anything like me, then I'm sure you're more than aware that individual investors are often anything but efficient. I first started investing as a young finance writer in my early 20s, when I was assigned a feature on online share dealing. I felt that I should go through the process myself, and trade a few stocks too, if I was to explain the ins and outs accurately to my readers. So I opened an account with one of the discount dealers, and invested in three companies. I bought an ATM operator (because it almost literally had a licence to print cash). I bought a company that made a revolutionary lightweight air cargo container that promised to slash costs for airlines (a better mousetrap! What could go wrong?). And I bought a company that made smallpox vaccine – the particular bio-terrorism scare story of the day.

I made lots of mistakes – I bought the stocks for the wrong reasons (I liked their 'stories' rather than their fundamentals), I failed to do my research diligently, and I had already rationalised away the nagging understanding that this laziness would likely cost me money, by mentally accounting for the sum I'd invested as a 'tuition fee'. In short, there was nothing rational about my decision-making process – and in the end, I took a loss on every one of those stocks, ranging from a couple of per cent to a 70% drop. And it served me right.

The market is 'kinda, sorta' efficient

However, the EMH persists for two main reasons. Firstly, lots of people have done a lot of work on it and a lot of the models that are used by analysts and others working in financial markets are dependent on it. So there is resistance to changing things drastically. You also need to come up with a better theory that can still be used to underpin corporate finance forecasts and models in the way that the EMH does.

But secondly, and most importantly, the EMH survives because at the end of the day, the market is at least 'kinda, sorta' efficient, even if you can't say the same for every individual investor. Markets don't get everything right and they don't price things in immediately by any means. But generally speaking, a transparent, liquid market with plenty of participants is going to give you a better idea of what something is worth than any other measure you can think of.

There's a very good reason for that – participants in a market get paid for bringing new and reliable information or analysis to the market. How? Well, if you buy a share today because your information makes you believe that its price should be higher, and you turn out to be right – i.e. your information is good – then in the long run you'll get paid (in the form of a higher share price) for bringing it to market. In other words, functioning, well-designed free markets offer a strong incentive to people to bring their best information and thinking to the table and share it around.

Why engineers get frustrated with the market

So I'm not here to try to bury or ridicule the EMH. That's ultimately an argument for academics that will unfold over decades to come. However, I don't think it's a helpful mental model for investors to adopt if they want to make money by beating the market, which is ultimately what we are trying to do. Even a watered-down version of the EMH sees periods of inefficiency as the exception, whereas in fact they are the rule – they are a function of the way that markets really work.

To find a better way of thinking about markets – a more accurate mental model – we need to address the biggest flaw in the EMH, and in a lot of investors' thinking about markets, which is this: it treats the market as an objective measuring device.

In effect, the EMH says that there is a reality out there, and the market prices assets based on an objective understanding of that reality. A flood of information – companies reporting sales and profit figures, the economy generating surveys and statistics, headlines, new laws – feeds into the market, which, via the wisdom of crowds, values an asset based on what currently available information says about its future prospects.

In short, 'reality' goes in at one end of the market and 'price' comes out at the other end. The market is nothing more than an information-processing machine – a cool-headed, objective observer, separate from the reality it measures. That's why the market is always right (or as right as it can ever be), and therefore not worth trying to beat.

I regularly see this belief reflected in emails from a specific group of *MoneyWeek* readers – retired engineers. Many of them think that, given enough information, investing should be easy, and are irritated to find that the market doesn't do what they expect. Their frustration is understandable. Engineers are practically minded, and are used to having a better grasp of how things work than most people. They approach the market as though it is a machine or a system. If they can just understand how cog 'A' drives cog 'B', then they will be able to invest accordingly and wait for the big pile of money to come out at the other end.

This approach works well if you are talking about a natural phenomenon like gravity. If you drop an apple, it will hit the ground. Your belief about why this happens is irrelevant – gravity doesn't care about your opinion. So given sufficient time, curiosity, imagination, and the application of the scientific method, you will eventually find a model that explains correctly and consistently why the apple hits the ground, and which can be used to make accurate predictions.

Unfortunately, financial markets are nothing like this.

A better view of markets, from the man who broke the Bank of England

So how does the market really work? There are many people – both professional investors and academics – working on this subject, particularly in the field of behavioural economics. But in terms of a broad framework on which to build your understanding of the market, one of the best I've read is the 'theory of reflexivity' put forward by George Soros. Soros has his detractors (his own son argues that he makes his investments based on intuition, then tries to rationalise his actions after the fact) but this is partly because his take on markets doesn't give investors any easy answers – it's not a 'plug-and-play' formula for making billions in the market.

But then, it's not meant to be. It's simply a more nuanced and realistic view of how markets work, which will put you in a better position to understand where opportunities for contrarian bets might exist, and which ones are worth pursuing. In any case, if you're going to listen to someone espouse an alternative philosophy of financial markets, then I struggle to see why you'd ignore the man who broke the Bank of England and made a billion dollars in the process, and who, by some measures, has an even better investment track record than the world's best-known investor, Warren Buffett.

The key improvement that Soros makes over the EMH is that he recognises that the relationship between markets and the underlying reality they are designed to measure is a two-way street. In other words, financial markets "can affect the future earnings flows they are supposed to reflect". For example, as property prices rise, banks become happier to lend money secured against property, which results in more money flowing into the sector, pushing values even higher, which in turn makes banks even more willing to lend.

And it's fair to say that the prevailing share price of a company has at least some impact on the average investor's view of what the share price 'should' be. By way of illustration, Keynes once compared the market to a beauty contest: imagine that a newspaper prints 100 photos, and offers a prize to the reader who gets closest to guessing the six photos that everyone else will pick as being the most attractive. In other words, your goal is not to pick the faces that you find most attractive, but those that you believe will "catch the fancy of the other competitors, all of whom are looking at the problem from the same point of view".

Keynes was complaining that rather than look at companies on their own merits and invest accordingly, investors spent all their time trying to outguess one another in their efforts to work out "what average opinion expects the average opinion to be". He didn't view this as a sensible way to allocate capital, but it was certainly a more clear-eyed view of markets than the EMH.

In short, markets help to shape the underlying reality, as well as the other way around. And because the two are constantly dancing a circle around one another, they never match up – there's always a gap between the model (the market) and reality. This is what Soros calls "reflexivity". In his 2014 book *Sapiens*, Yuval Noah Harari made a similar point, describing the market as a "second-order chaotic system" – a system that is not just complicated (as implied by the idea of 'chaos'), but one that also reacts to predictions about itself, and so can never be predicted accurately. For example, says Harari, what if you were to create a computer algorithm that everyone knew could predict tomorrow's oil price with 100% accuracy? The price would immediately rise to tomorrow's price – but then what would happen the following day?

To sum up, EMH suggests that the market puts prices on companies in much the way that a thermometer measures temperature. Soros (and market practitioners in general) understand that markets themselves are part of the system they measure, and so changes in the market will – through the actions of investors and companies – influence both future market prices and the fundamentals themselves. As a result, as Soros puts it, "market prices usually express a prevailing bias rather than the correct valuation".

Why it's better to assume that markets are always wrong

Now, most of the time, markets still perform their pricing function pretty well, even if it's not quite by the mechanism that the EMH predicts. That's because, in the normal course of things, incorrect views will be corrected when they bash up against reality. This is known as negative feedback. Given enough negative feedback, the market will have to find a new bias – one that reflects reality more accurately – until this bias in turn is challenged, and a new one has to be found. In short, negative feedback is a good thing. It "brings the participants' views and the actual situation closer together," notes Soros.

But, the existence of self-correcting negative feedback loops depends on one factor more than any other – diversity. As Michael Mauboussin points out, while individual market participants are anything but efficient, en masse there's a sufficiently diverse group of people and opinions to allow a wide range of potential outcomes to be priced in broadly accurately. It's this diversity that accounts for the 'wisdom of crowds'. In other words, a reasonably efficient market can still emerge out of the thought processes of a group of inefficient people – as long as they don't all think in the same way.

The problems arise when markets get caught up in a *positive* feedback loop. Positive feedback is self-reinforcing – it encourages market participants to continue doing what they are doing and believing what they are believing. Not only that, but other participants see the strategy working and adopt it too. At the extremes, this is how you get bubbles and busts (see chapter 10).

The most destructive positive feedback loops typically start with a good idea, as investors discover and exploit a genuinely profitable trend in the real world. For example, to continue the earlier example (which is one we're all too familiar with): let's say that house prices start rising, because interest rates are falling and it's becoming easier to get a mortgage. Investors who are early to the trend spot it, and profit from rising prices. Other investors note their peers getting rich, and jump on the trend too. As increasing amounts of money flow into the sector, the initial forces driving the trend lose their validity – house prices are no longer cheap relative to credit conditions, for example. But investors keep buying, because prices keep rising – and in turn, prices keep rising because investors keep buying. This, notes Soros, is why eventually "even valid interpretations of reality are bound to give rise to distorted ones" – because "ideas that work well will be overexploited to the point where they do not work anymore".

By this point, most investors who sat out the trade – and who might have provided the negative feedback required to close the gap between the markets and reality – have been roundly ignored and may even have given up. So the diversity that keeps markets relatively efficient has disappeared, and the market starts to price in a single outcome with an unwarranted level of certainty. In effect, the wisdom of crowds has degenerated into the madness of crowds. It's only when the gap between prices and reality is blatantly unsustainable (usually at a point well after the early investors and insiders have sold out) that the market comes crashing back to earth.

And while epoch-defining booms and busts are, by definition, rare, little pockets of inefficiency or areas where the gap between reality and the market are wide enough to be of interest to a sceptical investor are more common. We'll look at how to spot those in more detail later on in this book. The important thing to take away from this chapter is that, as Soros puts it, "markets may give the impression that they are always right, but the mechanism at work is very different from that implied by the prevailing paradigm".

If you can wrap your head around that, then you have a better chance of spotting and exploiting contrarian opportunities as they arise. And that's worth doing, because as Soros puts it: "generally speaking, the more an investment thesis is at odds with the generally prevailing view, the greater the financial rewards one can reap if it turns out to be correct". Indeed, it is far better to start from the view that "instead of being always right, financial markets are always wrong".

CHAPTER

3

*Why Should I
be a Sceptical
Investor?*

The best alternative to
sceptical investing – go passive

INVESTING IS HARD. There are no easy answers or straightforward prescriptions for identifying successful contrarian trades. As the great economist John Kenneth Galbraith said, "There is nothing reliable to be learned about making money. If there were, study would be intense and everyone with a positive IQ would be rich." Or as Warren Buffett's business partner Charlie Munger put it more recently: "It's not supposed to be easy. Anyone who finds it easy is stupid."

So what's the alternative? The obvious answer is 'passive' or 'index' investing, which takes the efficient market hypothesis to its logical conclusion. If markets are always roughly right, then there is no point in trying to beat them – you might as well just follow them, by replicating the underlying index. So if you are investing in UK stocks, you don't buy a fund run by a human being who tries to pick and choose individual winners ('active' investing). Instead, you just buy a fund that owns every share in the same proportions as the FTSE 350, and only makes changes to reflect the underlying index, rather than trying to beat it.

Jack Bogle, the founder of huge US asset manager Vanguard, set up the first mainstream index fund in 1975. Bogle recognised that investors as a group cannot beat the market, because they *are* the market. In fact, they must underperform the market, because their combined performance equals the market's performance, less fees. Therefore, most investors would be better off simply using an index (or passive) fund, which can charge lower fees than an active fund because it's cheaper and easier to run. In the City jargon, you get all the 'beta' (the return on the market) without paying for someone else's futile efforts to acquire 'alpha' (the return added by a skilled manager).

The logic is impeccable – and it works. Study after study shows that a large majority of active fund managers fail to beat their benchmark index over the long term, particularly once you take fees into account. Such is the power of the financial industry that it has taken a long time for passive funds to become significant competitors to active funds. But since the early 2000s – and following the 2008 financial crisis in particular – the amount of money being invested in passive funds has rocketed, helped by the growing popularity of exchange-traded funds (ETFs) – essentially index funds that are listed on the stock market. According to investment data provider Morningstar, by the end of 2017, passive index trackers and ETFs accounted for nearly 45% of assets under management in US stock markets, up from just 20% at the end of 2006. In other words, nearly half of the money invested in US stock market funds was passive, rather than active. And that share is only growing. In the UK, meanwhile, around a quarter of assets under management were invested in passive funds by the end of 2016, versus around 17% in 2007.

Most objections to passive investing come from vested interests

Naturally, the financial services industry has plenty of objections to passive investment. Active fund managers and other intermediaries (research analysts, investment consultants and the like) ultimately derive their profits from investors' efforts to grow their money more rapidly than the market. If investors wake up to the fact that they can get better returns at lower prices simply by not trying, then that's a disaster for the active fund management industry. As a result, the active management lobby has queued up to denounce the flow of 'dumb money' that passive funds have funnelled into the market.

The problem for active managers is that they can't challenge the weight of data which shows that very few of them actually beat the market consistently. So instead we've seen objections levelled at a philosophical or even ethical level. For example, one US brokerage – Sanford C. Bernstein – compared passive investment unfavourably to communist central planning, in a 2016 paper entitled 'The Silent Road to Serfdom: Why Passive Investing is Worse than Marxism'. The argument here is that the social purpose of markets is to allocate resources efficiently. Individuals make decisions about the best place to put their money for the best returns, and that combined wisdom channels it to where it will be most productively used. Under Marxism, this system is replaced with central planning, which is inefficient but is at least an attempt to allocate resources.

But with passive investing, argue the authors of the report, there is no attempt to allocate capital at all – individuals just blindly pile into whichever stocks happen to be at the top of the index. For markets to work, it takes active investors working hard to allocate capital sensibly. The passive investors are just "free riders" – and if they put the active investors out of business, we'll be left with the blind leading the blind.

Others argue that passive investment undermines competition. If you own every stock in an index or sector, you don't actually want them to compete with one another – you'd rather they formed a cartel and pushed up prices. Still others argue that passive investors are unable to hold management teams to account effectively – they lack the ultimate sanction of being able to sell shares in companies whose actions they disapprove of.

Passive investing is one of the best financial innovations in history

So what does passive investing mean for a sceptical investor? The obvious argument, and one that many active managers make, is that the rise of passive investing should make life easier for active investors, because it will result in more inefficiencies and thus opportunities to beat the market. After all, if the 'dumb money' is blindly rushing into passive funds and abetting the misallocation of capital, then surely that's good news for the 'smart' money active fund managers?

This argument sounds good, and logical, and it'd save me a lot of work if I just went along with it – 'the crowd is blindly piling into passive investing right now, so there's never been a better time to be a contrarian'. But while it's a superficially appealing argument, those are exactly the sorts of arguments we should be sceptical of, because they're usually wrong. Particularly if they're being put about by people who have a vested interest in them being true.

The truth is, I'm a big fan of passive investing. The financial industry has been ripping investors off with promises they can't keep and fees they can't justify for decades. Managers are only panicking now and talking about their 'social purpose' because passive funds jeopardise the high-fee, low-effort business models they have been getting away with for too long. On average, passive funds charge less and deliver better returns, and that is a far better deal for most investors than the one we've been getting from the financial industry. You cannot argue with that.

The objection that passive investing encourages the blind allocation of capital is fair in theory. But a lot of this capital was already being blindly allocated – many of the 'active' funds now losing assets to passive funds were closet trackers in any case (funds that charge active fees but deliver near-market returns by hugging their underlying index as tightly as possible). So in many cases, investors have merely swapped an expensive closet tracker for a cheaper genuine tracker. As for the efficiency argument, the big question – to which no one has the answer – is *how much active management do we actually need?* Given the failings of the industry, I suspect the answer is 'a lot less than we currently have'.

As for the idea that passive funds can't hold managements to account, active funds have hardly been great exemplars of that, as the soaring size of executive pay packets demonstrates. A good example is the 2018 scandal of housebuilder Persimmon, whose chief executive Jeff Fairburn resigned after the outcry that arose from him being paid a (reduced) bonus of around £75m under the terms of a long-term incentive plan. This pay deal was voted through by most fund manager owners of the stock in 2012, despite the UK Shareholders' Association warning very clearly of the egregious nature of the package. Equally, passive managers are starting to take corporate governance a lot more seriously – increasingly voting against managements and using their clout to discourage companies from issuing share classes that strip voting rights from shareholders.

There's more to passive investing than market capitalisation

Underlying all this is a big semantic problem. When people decry passive investing, they usually mean one specific form of passive investing – buying into the big stock market indices, which are weighted by market capitalisation. But these are far from the only forms of passive investment.

There are sector funds that invest in one specific industry. Or 'smart beta' indices, which aim to invest in stocks with certain qualities (or 'factors') that tend to outperform over time (so you might have an index based on momentum stocks or value stocks). These funds are effectively duplicating active strategies but using a passive framework.

In short, the vast majority of objections to index investing consist of self-interested carping from an active industry that would rather circle the wagons than address the shortcomings of its own flawed business model, and you should mostly ignore them.

The metagame and the one thing that doesn't change

So am I saying that sceptical investors should just go with the flow, forget trying to beat the market, and embrace pure passive investing? Not at all. But we do need to consider – free from industry propaganda – how the rise of passive investing is likely to affect the market and the opportunities that it might open up. This is where I want to introduce a useful concept – the **metagame**.

When playing games that involve both strategy and luck (poker, for example), if you want to win consistently you have to take account of elements that are outwith the rules of the game itself. For example, you can be a brilliant technical poker player and have a perfect grip on the odds of getting the various different hands. But if you don't pay attention to what's going on in the heads of the players around you – their ability to bluff and so on – then you will struggle to beat them. This is the 'metagame'.

So how does the metagame work in investment? The key is in understanding what changes and what remains the same. The mechanisms of investing, the specific technologies that everyone is excited about, the politics of the day – all of these things change. The layout of the board, if you like, is always different. Where sceptics can gain an edge is by understanding how the one constant – human behaviour – interacts with these changes.

Warren Buffett's outstanding investment record, argues Shane Parrish of the Farnam Street blog, largely "comes from identifying the constraints of others and capitalising on those structural disadvantages". For example, says Parrish, Buffett recognises the psychological pressures and skewed incentives that a public listing imposes on managers. So he prefers to take his companies private, which allows the management team to focus on long-term value creation for the ultimate benefit of its owner – who happens to be Buffett. By understanding at a high level how human nature interacts with the rules of the system, Buffett gets the best out of the companies he owns by side-stepping the normal structures. As Parrish puts it: "If you follow the norms of the system, the results you get are likely to be the norm. When you play a different game, a metagame, you have the opportunity to outperform."

In short, the contours of the environment in which humans operate in terms of incentives, financial structures and technological developments, shift all the time. When people say: 'It's different this time', it often is. But the one thing that does not change is human behaviour. As a sceptical investor, you can use that understanding to figure out how human behaviour is likely to interact with today's changing environment to create opportunities.

The metagame and passive investing

So how can we apply this idea to passive investing? Here are three simple rules of thumb regarding human behaviour which we can use to think about how the rise of passive investing might affect our own investments.

RULE I: STABILITY
BREEDS INSTABILITY

As Soros points out, human nature being what it is, we always push a good thing to its limits and then beyond – we break it. Pretty much every bubble in history has been caused or at least abetted by a hot new financial technology being pushed to breaking point, from collective investment structures to complex derivatives to asset-backed bonds. Right now, passive investing is the hot new financial technology. As a result, the amount of money flooding into it, and the level of technical innovation, is growing. It's already clear that passive investing is having an impact on the way that money flows into and around markets. When the big index providers change the composition of their indices, that change is felt in global stock markets. In other words, some stocks are bought or sold purely on the basis of how an index provider classifies them – 'fundamentals' play no part whatsoever in this movement.

At some point, this will overreach itself, and passive funds and ETFs will end up playing a role in the next financial crisis. If that does happen, it will most likely be the result of lots of people investing in a fund that they think does one thing, but which turns out to be exposed to a completely different set of risks from the ones they had prepared for. For example, if you invest in a cheap S&P 500 tracker, you know what you'll end up getting, and it's hard to see a situation in which the existence of such funds does much real damage to the system (beyond making the swings bigger when a crash does come). But if you buy a low-volatility, multi-asset, rum-and-raisin-flavoured smart beta ETF, for example, then it's trickier to understand the rules involved.

(Yes, I'm being a little facetious here, but with more than 3.3m indices in existence it's only a matter of time before ice cream flavours come into play.)

RULE 2: FOLLOW THE MONEY

We'll look at incentives in more detail in chapter 8. But a useful point to remember about innovative new products is that in the early days, the interests of consumers and product providers are often closely linked. The provider gains market share by creating a product that serves the needs of consumers better than the incumbents. Everybody's happy. But as the sector grows and evolves, the interests of consumers and providers often diverge. What is profitable may no longer reflect what is best for the consumer.

Here's an example from the world of ETFs. Many smart beta ETFs own many of the same underlying stocks, even though they all claim to be using different strategies. As Howard Marks of Oaktree Capital points out, this is at least in part because of the skewed incentives at work. ETF providers need scale (if you are charging 0.1% a year, you need to be charging that on a big pile of money to make any profit), and that means owning stocks that are big enough to accommodate a lot of passive money. Ultimately passive providers are no different to the traditional fund management industry – they want to gather as many assets as possible, and this goal is not always perfectly in line with the customer's aim of generating the best investment performance possible. So the ease of selling a particular idea (which usually reflects the popularity rather than the attractiveness of a strategy) may dictate the product creation process more than the effectiveness of the underlying approach.

Eventually, the risk is that every new ETF becomes just another way to funnel money into the most popular stocks. The more that this happens, the further the market drifts from reflecting the fundamentals of companies, towards anticipating the likely direction of future investment flows from index funds – creating a 'positive feedback loop' in reflexivity terms. It also leaves the entire market structurally vulnerable to changes in the outlook for the biggest companies.

RULE 3: FAMILIARITY BREEDS CONTEMPT (FOR RISK)

Finally, there is a danger that passive investors become complacent. As Marks puts it, he struggles with passive investing because he can't imagine asking a client "how happy he is about investing in stocks that no one is analysing". This isn't echoing the 'Marxism' argument about blind allocation of capital – it's more the concern that investors decide that they don't even need to understand what their funds are investing in. It's one thing to accept your limitations as an active investor, but that's quite different to completely abdicating any responsibility for your money.

We know that when investors cede responsibility, they stop paying attention. Aaron Brask, formerly of Barclays, compares the risks of passive investing with the subprime crisis that precipitated the Great Recession of 2008, in a piece by Kopin Tan for US paper *Barron's*. "When investors stopped conducting their own due diligence and started relying on rating agencies, it opened the door for capital misallocation, and ultimately culminated in the credit crisis." The equivalent danger today could be the role that unquestioning passive investors – who are, as Jim Grant of

Grant's Interest Rate Observer puts it, "price-insensitive buyers" – have played in driving equity markets to unprecedented levels of overvaluation.

What are the implications of all this?

The structure of passive investments, and investor enthusiasm for them, suggests that the big companies that are included in many indices are probably over-owned. Some investors hold them for no other reason than that lots of other investors own them. There is therefore likely to be more scope for such companies to suffer big drops in their share price if they disappoint investors, as feedback loops form (investors selling merely because other investors are selling). It also implies that companies without much exposure to passive indices are likely under-owned relative to their valuations.

There is already evidence that this is happening. A study by Vincent Deluard of INTL FCStone found that the more indices a stock was featured in, the more expensive it tended to be, relative to those that were underrepresented in indices. By way of example, value investors Murray Stahl and Steven Bregman of Horizon Kinetics argue that mature stocks, such as oil giant Exxon and fast food group McDonald's, have for several years now, been propped up – to an extent unjustified by their fundamentals – by this constant inflow of capital. As Bregman put it in the 30 November 2018 issue of *Value Investor Insight*, "what we consider inefficient pricing ... in stocks like this has to do with automatic buying driven by inflows into passive vehicles". Meanwhile, companies that are locked out of indices due to limited liquidity or an unusual corporate structure "have effectively been rendered invisible". All of this may take time to reverse – but, then, patience is a vital trait for any sceptical investor.

More generally, it makes sense for wary investors to monitor the ETF sector for signs of stress and over-exuberance. Prior to 2008, we saw plenty of stress in parts of the hedge fund industry and other more obscure funds before anything disastrous happened to the wider financial system. If the market starts to run into trouble, we might expect to see some early warning signs in the ETF sector beforehand – funds shutting down, not behaving as they should (failing to track their underlying index, for example), or apparently unconnected funds behaving in similar ways.

A final problem with passive investing, is that contrarianism is ultimately about doing something different to the broader market. I like passive investing. But the more that everyone views the world through the same lens, the more valuable becomes the "variant perception" (as hedge fund giant Michael Steinhardt calls it) that sceptics try to cultivate.

What's the alternative?

If you'd rather not take a view on the market at all, you could opt to invest as passively as you can. You could buy a global equity tracker, a global bond tracker, and shift your money between them according to risk preference (indeed, Lars Kroijer, a former hedge fund manager turned passive investment evangelist, has written a good book explaining this whole thesis). Alternatively, a good investment adviser (or even 'robo-adviser' these days) will be able to put together a cheap portfolio of tracker funds to suit your needs. This is as close as you'll get to genuinely passive investment – you are effectively getting exposure to the entire market of asset classes out there, and you're happy to take an overall market return.

There is nothing at all wrong with that. And nor is it a case of all or nothing. It's fine to have the core of your portfolio invested in a simple tracker portfolio and then to experiment with your other investments. Part of your money can be passive and part of it can be betting on contrarian outcomes.

However, as we've already pointed out, the term 'passive' is a misnomer. You're always making some sort of active choice. Even your decision to buy a given index at a given time is an active decision. And there's nothing to stop sceptical investors from using passive funds. If Japan is cheap and everyone hates it, for example, and you decide to buy it, then it doesn't matter whether you invest in the market via a passive index fund, or an actively managed investment trust, or a selection of individual Japanese shares – it doesn't make the trade any less contrarian.

In short, you have to make judgements, regardless of how simple and hands-off your portfolio is. And you'll do a better job of making those judgements if you learn how to be a more sceptical investor. The good news is that you, as an individual investor, have a massive advantage over institutional investors and fund managers, as we'll see in the next chapter.

CHAPTER

4

*Your Big
Advantage Over the
Professionals*

I N EARLY JULY 2007, stock markets around the world were approaching new highs or challenging those last seen before the technology bubble burst back in 2000. To look solely at a chart of stocks, you might have assumed that all was right with the world. But there was unease in the air. Few people openly acknowledged it, or even fully understood it, but the credit crunch was already well underway. US house prices – which had replaced tech stocks as the investment mania of the day – had long since stopped going up. Indeed, they were falling across the nation (which, according to Ben Bernanke, then head of the Federal Reserve, had never happened before), and as a result, the full extent of the careless lending that took hold during the boom was being revealed.

In February 2007, banking giant HSBC had issued its first ever profit warning, hit by unexpectedly large losses at its US subprime mortgages unit. In April, New Century, one of the biggest subprime lenders, filed for bankruptcy protection. In June, investment bank Bear Stearns had to step in to save two of its hedge funds from subprime-related losses. And within a few short months, the front pages in Britain would be filled with photos of customers queuing in fear for their savings, as building-society-turned-aggressive-mortgage-lender Northern Rock's funding dried up and Britain saw its first bank run since the panic that came in the wake of the collapse of the City of

Glasgow Bank in 1878 (other banks had gone bust in the interim period, but not quite as visibly). In short, the end was nigh.

But for now, the worries could be dismissed. When was the market not fretting about something? Times were still good. The Federal Reserve was reassuring everyone that the subprime crisis would be "contained". And stocks were still rising. Nothing summed up the atmosphere of that early summer more than a now infamous interview by the *Financial Times* with Chuck Prince, then chief executive of US investment bank Citigroup (since rebranded as the more PR-friendly 'Citi'). Citigroup had been one of the most prolific lenders to private equity groups, and *FT* journalists Michiyo Nakamoto and David Wighton gently asked Prince whether Citigroup was considering pulling in its horns a bit, given the spreading jitters in the credit markets. Prince denied it would be a problem. That market was a lot more liquid than it once was, he argued. "A disruptive event now needs to be much more disruptive than it used to be." Then came the killer quote. "When the music stops, in terms of liquidity, things will be complicated. But as long as the music is playing, you've got to get up and dance. We're still dancing."

As it turned out, Prince had to stop dancing rather abruptly just a few months later. He stepped down as chief executive in November, as it transpired that Citi had a lot more exposure to subprime mortgages than anyone had quite realised. His 'dancing' quote is now regularly cited as an example of executive hubris at its worst.

Here's why the professionals can't stop dancing

But, in fact, I'd argue that Prince's quote is one of the most insightful and (perhaps unwittingly) honest comments on the nature of the financial industry ever made by someone in his position. Everyone in the financial industry – from banks to wealth managers to advisers to journalists – makes money from activity. If markets are going wild and providing opportunities to reap fees from lending and advising, or everyone else is coining it by being fully invested in the market, then you had better be involved or your clients are going to wonder why you're not making money when all the other banks and funds are. As blogger Yves Smith (of the Naked Capitalism blog) noted at the time of Prince's interview, anyone in the industry who bails out of a roaring market too early will be in trouble. "They will lose their place in the league tables and, if they manage money, will suffer in performance rankings."

An example that's perhaps closer to home is the cautionary tale of Paul Moore, who joined HBOS as head of group regulatory risk in 2002. In 2004, Moore warned the board that the bank's sales culture was too aggressive and had to be reined in. He was sacked for his pains. Four years later, HBOS had to be bailed out by the government, after a forced merger with Lloyds went wrong and dragged the latter bank under too.

That's what happens when you work in financial services during a boom and you stop dancing. Even though Moore was proved right in the end, his stance cost him a great deal of personal suffering – and not every whistleblower ends up being vindicated as publicly or completely as Moore was. So even if a City worker had concerns, you can see why they might not feel there was much benefit to acting on them. Better to wait until the market panic begins. Even if you can't get out before everyone else does, you'll all go down on the same ship – so your own errors will be obscured by everyone else's.

Reluctant bulls and fully invested bears

You might think that this sounds overly cynical or illogical. Why invest in assets that you know to be overvalued or at risk of blowing up? But it makes perfect sense when you look at the incentives that drive the biggest players in markets. Take fund managers. What's the most important thing for the average active fund manager? You might think 'their performance'. You'd be wrong. The average fund manager gets paid based on the amount of money he or she is managing. So the primary goal is to increase the quantity of assets under management.

Don't get me wrong – fund performance is an important factor. If a fund has done well, it'll generally attract more investors. But it's also easier to attract assets by being in a 'hot' sector. And woe betide you if you deliberately avoid a sector that stubbornly continues to make money. Even if you are eventually proved right, no one will thank you for it. In turn, all of this pressure gives rise to the type of investor known as the 'fully invested bear'.

Jeremy Grantham, the co-founder of US-based wealth manager GMO, tells a great story about the tech bubble. As 'value' investors, GMO had avoided technology stocks, feeling unable to justify investing their clients' money in companies with no profits, frequently no sales either, and business plans that were often dubious or at best somewhat flimsy. The company had suffered for its decision to sit out the tech bubble. Clients pulled their money out as they saw friends or rivals making huge paper profits on soaring tech stocks, while their 'cheap' stocks made far more pedestrian gains.

Grantham found it hard to believe that he was the only one who thought that tech stocks were overvalued. So in 1998 and 1999, with the market trading at extremely high valuations, he surveyed roughly 1,100 professional investors, asking them to answer just two simple questions.

First, he asked: if market valuations were to fall back to their average levels within a decade, would it guarantee a major bear market? Every one of the respondents replied "Yes". His second question was simple: do you believe that markets will return to average valuations over that time period? All but seven – so, 99% – of the respondents said "Yes".

In other words, the vast majority of fund managers believed there was a bubble, that it would burst, and that, when it did burst, their clients would lose a lot of money. Yet they were buying tech stocks anyway, because if they didn't clients would pull their money out of the funds and the managers would get fired. This short-termism means that fund managers as a whole are both less patient and less radical in their investments than individual investors. As John Maynard Keynes put it, "Worldly wisdom teaches that it is better for reputation to fail conventionally than to succeed unconventionally".

The upside of
career risk

This is what is sometimes known as 'career risk'. And it is yet another factor that results in a huge gap appearing between the market's view of reality and what's really happening on the ground. Even professional contrarian investors find it hard to resist. In his 1994 book, *Five Eminent Contrarians*, Steven L. Mintz spoke to Michael Aronstein of Comstock Partners. A contrarian has to be flexible, said Aronstein, and yet investors "would like you to lay still and let them call you a growth manager or an asset allocater or an interest-rate timer ... The system is just designed to channel money to people who make themselves easy to understand. You get the money because of the way in which people can categorise you, and secondarily because it was successful."

Yet while it's a major problem for those who work in the finance industry, career risk is a massive bonus for you as an individual investor. As Michael Mauboussin notes, there are two major hurdles to being contrarian. One hurdle is the range of psychological tics that affect anyone who tries to go against the consensus – those affect us all, and we'll talk about them in chapter 6. But the other hurdle is institutional – and it only affects those who work in the business. In effect, whatever a fund manager says about being an independent thinker when he's being interviewed by the financial press, the reality is that the financial services business is structurally biased against genuine contrarians. Being a contrarian fund manager is a thankless task and one that positively threatens your livelihood. As Grantham put it, in the asset management business, "you can't deliver the hard truth and prosper ... if you're right on your own it's a bit dangerous; when you are wrong on your own, you will not receive much mercy."

What's bad news for fund managers is great news for you

But that just leaves more opportunity for the private investor. You don't have to be a 'fully invested bear'. You don't have to worry about 'career risk'. You don't have to answer to any investment committees or family offices or to anyone or anything but your own sense of pride. That freedom is the edge you have over the City and Wall Street – the freedom not to invest, not to do what everyone else is doing simply because they are doing it; the freedom to take a more sceptical approach.

As Allan Mecham, the highly respected head of Arlington Value Management, puts it: "This is where the individual investor has a huge advantage over the professional; most fund managers don't have the leeway to patiently wait for the exceptional opportunity." (It's also why, if you decide to invest with an active manager, you should be going for smaller funds – the bigger players are practically incentivised to manage your money in a mediocre manner. But I'll talk more about that in chapter 15.)

Of course, you still have to overcome the psychological obstacles to investing sceptically. And that's what we'll address in the next few chapters.

CHAPTER

5

You Versus the Crowd

W E'VE JUST DISCUSSED how fear of being fired drives professional fund managers to conform. And their main rivals – the passive funds – encourage herding behaviour by definition. So there are a lot of forces in investment – from apathy to peer pressure – that push individuals to run with the crowd. That should spell opportunity for those who go against the crowd.

The one problem – and it's a big one – is that even though you know this, you will still struggle to escape your own desire to run with the herd when you are thinking or investing. In this chapter, I want to explain why this is, and what you can do about it.

A simple model for crowd behaviour

As with any complex system, you can't model the human mind perfectly. We're a morass of conflicting, shifting desires affected by changes in both our internal environment (our own biochemistry) and our interactions with our external environment (other people, the weather, what's on the telly). But we don't need to go into complicated models of individual minds to get a good idea of how crowds work. There are just two key impulses to wrap your head around.

They're commonly described as 'greed' and 'fear'. But I'm not so keen on those labels – both have very negative connotations. I prefer to say we have an **expansionary** impulse and a **contractionary** one. When you are in an expansionary mood, your focus is on growing your wealth, grabbing a bigger piece of the cake, empire-building. When you are in contractionary mode, you want to hunker down, build walls, protect what is yours. These two impulses are in turn driven by one simple fact: the knowledge that, one day, you will be dead.

A matter of life or death

When evolutionary psychologists and behavioural economists talk about what drives our herding instincts, they often hark back to the days when we were dwelling in Stone Age tribes out on the African savannah, at constant risk of being picked off by lions, dying of dehydration, or nibbling on some poisonous vegetation. The idea is that we are programmed to run with the crowd because it's safer.

But there's more to it than a simple evolutionary hangover. You really don't have to go back to the Stone Age to find unforgiving death lurking around every corner. Vaccines and antibiotics only became widely available to most people (in developed countries at that) in the middle of the last century. In 1924, four years before the discovery of penicillin, the 16-year-old son of one of the most powerful men in the world – US president Calvin Coolidge – died of septicaemia that resulted from a blister that developed on his toe while he was playing tennis in ill-fitting shoes.

Even today, and even in the most advanced societies, life is unpredictable and full of potentially lethal threats. And while all animals have a 'fight or flight' instinct when faced with life-threatening situations, only humans (as far as we can tell) have a sufficiently evolved brain to bless us with an ever-present awareness of the inevitability of our own extinction. This fear may not always be at the forefront of our minds, but it's never far away.

What does any fundamentally rational being crave in such an environment? It's not happiness or contentment (although these may be desirable side effects). It's security and certainty. I want to keep myself and my loved ones safe, and I also want to know that after I am gone, the things that I value will persist (it doesn't matter that I'll be gone at that point – what matters is how I feel about that now, while I'm alive). To do that, I need to be able to do two things. I need to get out there and explore and master my environment in order to take advantage of opportunities that could make my life better and my situation more secure (the expansionary impulse), but I also need to be highly alert to danger and ready to raise my defences in response to threats to that security (the contractionary impulse).

Building and defending our models of the world

So how do we navigate an uncertain world? How do we impose order on the chaos around us? It's simple. We look for elements that appear to be predictable – we seek patterns. We look for cause-and-effect rules that govern outcomes and can be used to influence them. If we know (or at least think we know) that 'x' causes 'y', then we can increase our level of certainty in our world view.

Some rules are governed by natural phenomenon – don't fall off cliffs; don't eat poisonous mushrooms. Some are instinctive (social animals such as humans and apes have been found to have an inherent sense of 'fairness', even though the world itself is clearly not naturally 'fair'). But many of the most important ones are social (such as learning the conventions for crossing a road or transacting with one another).

And the critical point is that we don't formulate these world views alone. They are passed down from our parents, and reinforced by our schools, friends, co-religionists and colleagues. In fact, historian Yuval Noah Harari, in his recent bestselling book *Sapiens*, argues that this ability to create and believe in epic, society-spanning shared world views – from religions to legal systems to money itself (which ultimately derives its value from our belief in it, and the social structures that give everyone the confidence to rely upon it) – is key to our spectacular success as a species.

You can call them stories, as Harari does, or you can call them social structures, or you can think of them as rules for a particularly complicated board game. But however you describe them, they are all systems that human beings have invented to enable us to cooperate in a more mutually beneficial way – and our brains are wired to be receptive to information presented like this.

Terror management theory and investing

The thing is, natural rules work regardless of how you feel about them – you don't argue with gravity. But social structures only work because everyone buys into them. Your shared values keep you safe. The values of others could disrupt the social cohesion that underwrites that sense of safety. Note that it doesn't matter whether adopting another set of values might improve your life – leaving your 'tribe' incurs definite costs in return for uncertain gains, so switching out of a world view that has so far proved relatively successful is a huge risk. And make no mistake – the psychological stakes are extremely high. It really is a matter of life or death.

The idea that the awareness of our own mortality has a major impact on our behaviour – "terror management theory" – was pioneered by Abram Rosenblatt and Jeff Greenberg of the University of Arizona, building on the ideas of anthropologist Ernest Becker. And countless studies (outlined in a very readable book, *The Worm at the Core* by Sheldon Solomon, Greenberg and Tom Pyszczynski) have shown how it affects our actions.

On the one hand, thoughts of death make us defend our existing world view and cultural standards more aggressively against 'outside' views. In a 1987 experiment, for example, a group of municipal court judges in the US were asked to set bail for a hypothetical case in which a woman had been charged with prostitution. Half of the judges were given a questionnaire probing their beliefs and feelings about death before doing so, while the others were not. The latter group set bail at $50, the average for the crime at the time. Those judges who had been 'primed' with thoughts of death, however, set a far higher average bail of $455. In other words, a simple reminder of their mortality drove the judges to uphold the moral standards of their culture more aggressively. In another experiment, noted Greenberg in a 2012 interview with the *Atlantic*, "simply subliminally flashing the word 'death' on a computer screen to Americans for 28 milliseconds is enough to amplify negative reactions to an author who criticizes the US." In short, notes Greenberg, "when death is close to mind … people become more adamant in their beliefs … They increase prejudice and aggression against others who are different."

It also works the other way around. In another study, Canadian subjects were asked to read essays that either belittled Canadian society or Australian society. They were then asked to play a specially designed anagram game. The subjects who had read the attack on their own values produced more death-related words in the anagram game than those who had read the attack on Australia. In other words, having their world view attacked brought thoughts of death and vulnerability closer to the surface.

Look at it this way and you can see why we have such a strong desire to go along with the 'in group' and be sceptical or downright hostile towards the 'out group'. You need only look at the tone of the debate over something like Brexit, or Donald Trump to see just how aggressive or histrionic people can become when they feel that their fundamental world view is being challenged in some way. It's because we view it literally as a matter of mortal peril.

What this means
for investment

What implications does this have for investment psychology and for sceptical investing in particular? Firstly, our desire for certainty and acceptance discourages us from going against the prevailing wisdom, particularly when it's espoused by 'people like us'. So when other investors are in expansionary mode – when they're feeling greedy – we want to do the same, because we don't want to miss out or get left behind. Similarly, when they're in contractionary mode – when they're afraid – we'd rather be on the same side too. Ultimately the market expresses a number of competing world views – as participants in the market it's our natural desire to get on the same side as the most dominant one. As Gustave Le Bon wrote in his 1895 book, *Psychologie des foules* (*The Crowd*): "Ideas, sentiments, emotions, and beliefs possess in crowds a contagious power as intense as that of microbes."

Secondly, our instinctive pattern-spotting and craving for explanations makes us suckers for a good story. Stories are after all, just large, complicated patterns – convincingly embroidered tapestries of cause and effect. Some are based on fundamental data; others are constructed after the fact to explain a market movement that's already happened; and most are a combination of the two. This tendency is something that Nobel-winning Yale finance professor Robert Shiller calls the "narrative fallacy". In his 2017 paper, 'Narrative Economics', he points out that "the human brain has always been highly tuned towards narratives, whether factual or not, to justify ongoing actions, even such basic actions as spending and investing. Stories motivate and connect activities to deeply felt values and needs." Indeed, Shiller believes that "the prevalence and vividness of certain stories" may even have more bearing on the length and depth of a recession, say, than specific economic factors (as people react to their belief in stories by amending their behaviour accordingly).

Four ways to remain apart from the crowd

As investment author and analyst Michael Mauboussin points out, a good contrarian has to be ready to go "against the crowd when the gap between fundamentals and expectations warrants it." That's hard enough, but it's made harder by the fact that "the widest gap often coincides with the strongest urge to be part of the group ... prices not only inform investors, they also influence investors". In short, the desire to be part of the in group, and the potency of the stories that have been constructed to back up its world view, are hardest to resist, just when a more sceptical opinion is likely to prove most valuable. So how do you resist falling in with the crowd?

I. GET COMFORTABLE WITH BEING UNCOMFORTABLE

Jeremy Grantham, co-founder of US asset manager GMO, built a behavioural investment model with his colleague Ben Inker (using US stocks) to try to explain why the price that investors are willing to pay for a given level of earnings (the price/earnings ratio) goes up and down over time. Their goal was to find out what characteristics make investors more willing to buy the market at higher P/Es.

One thing to remember when considering this is that corporate profit margins tend to be 'mean reverting' over the long run. This is a critical feature of free market capitalism (and one which many argue has been undermined by the recent long period of low interest rates, although that discussion is beyond the scope of this book). If one company makes unusually high profits in a sector, other entrepreneurs will target the opportunity too. The resulting competition drives profit margins down.

So when margins are unusually high, rational investors operating in an efficient market should be reluctant to pay a high P/E, because they know that profits should fall in the future. Similarly, when margins are low relative to the long-term average, investors should be willing to buy at higher P/Es, because they know that the 'E' side of the equation is due to rise in the near future.

That, of course, is not what Grantham and Inker found. Instead, they found that investors are much keener to buy stocks when profit margins are high. "Investors would dependably pay up for high margins, which would then decline, whacking them on the way down." Investors also pay more when inflation is low and GDP growth is relatively stable. In short, the closer to perfect that economic and corporate conditions are, the more investors are willing to pay for a given level of earnings. They want to see blue skies everywhere before they buy, despite history proving over and over again that grey clouds inevitably darken blue skies, and that peak profits inevitably decline. It's almost as though they imagine that this time, the good times will last forever, and tomorrow will look almost exactly like today, only better.

Grantham describes these features – high margins, low inflation, stable growth – as "comfort factors", and points out that human beings will pay a high premium for them, and always have (at least, going back to 1925, which is where GMO's model ends). "Investors' extreme preference for comfort, like human nature, has never changed." This desire for comfort and fear of discomfort, says Grantham, explains all of the bubbles and troughs during that period (except 2000, when US stocks were even more overvalued than "comfort factors" would explain alone). When you combine this finding with Greenberg's "terror management theory", it makes perfect sense. Investors want everything around them to confirm that they are making the right choice before they take a risk. But this craving is a disaster when applied to something as cyclical as financial markets. Investors' tendency to extrapolate today's conditions far into the future means that the expansionary impulse is strongest when conditions can't possibly get any better – which is, of course, precisely the point at which you should be in full-blown contractionary mode, consolidating your gains before the next storm hits.

So get used to feeling uncomfortable. As Howard Marks of Oaktree Capital puts it: "Most great investments begin in discomfort. The things most people feel good about – investments where the underlying premise is widely accepted, the recent performance has been positive and the outlook is rosy – are unlikely to be available at bargain prices. Rather, bargains are usually found among things that are controversial, that people are pessimistic about, and that have been performing badly of late. But it isn't easy to do things that entail discomfort." Or as financial writer and adviser Barry Ritholtz puts it: "Easy trades are rarely lucrative ones."

In short, you want to be risking money when your gut and heart are stuck in defensive, fearful contractionary mode, and you want to be very careful of having money at risk when your gut is in greedy expansion mode, and screaming at you to buy. As contrarian manager Ned Davis put it: "What feels right, easy, and obvious in your gut is quite often wrong."

2 . YOU WILL NEVER BE POPULAR – CULTIVATE MENTAL TOUGHNESS

In the fairytale, 'The Emperor's New Clothes', there's a reason it has to be a child who ends up pointing out that the emperor has no clothes on – it's because most adults have long since realised that it's more pleasant to be wrong and part of the 'in' crowd, than right and isolated. Where the fairytale got it wrong is in the idea that people are grateful or happy when their mistaken ideas are challenged or even proved wrong. People will do just about anything to defend their point of view.

To take a financial example, when the Queen asked of the financial crisis of 2008, "Why did no one see it coming?", a truthful answer from establishment economists would have gone something along the lines of: 'Well, actually, a lot of people did, but we didn't listen to them because incorporating their views would have meant ripping up everything we have to assume in order to make economics work (in theory).' Instead, the same people who missed that crisis because they had no understanding of, or interest in, the role that debt plays in our financial system are still trotting out much the same claptrap in academic papers and broadsheets across the land today.

This is a well-documented phenomenon known as *motivated ignorance*. It turns out that people's desire to be part of a 'shared reality' is so strong that they'll go out of their way to avoid hearing an opinion that disagrees with their strongly held views. In one study by researchers led by Jeremy Frimer and Matt Motyl at the University of Winnipeg, published in the *Journal of Experimental Social Psychology*, 200 people were asked to read an essay and then answer questions on same-sex marriage. They could choose to read the view they agreed with, or to read the opposing view. If they read the opinion they agreed with, they were entered into a raffle to win $7. If they read the opposition essay, they were entered into a raffle to win $10. It looks like a no-brainer – one option clearly offers a better prize for the same amount of effort (reading an essay) with no obvious downside. In a narrowly rational world, no one should have opted for the $7 option. Yet, in fact, 63% went for it. In other words, nearly two-thirds of the respondents preferred to have their views unchallenged, rather than have the chance of winning more money. Those on both "left and right," the study concludes, "are motivated to avoid hearing from the other side for some of the same reasons: the anticipation of cognitive dissonance [the unpleasant sensation of discomfort you get when your brain is trying to reconcile two conflicting points of view] and the undermining of a fundamental need for a shared reality with other people." As George Orwell put it back in 1945: "People can foresee the future only when it coincides with their own wishes, and the most grossly obvious facts can be ignored when they are unwelcome."

So you need to be able to put up with the fact that, even when (if) you are proved right in your scepticism, there will be no lasting plaudits, only financial rewards. People would rather be wrong, and emotionally comfortable, than allow you to upset their world view (which, after all, they perceive as a mortal threat). And if you ever put a foot wrong again, they will be waiting to pounce and to point out your errors, as a way of demonstrating that their world view is superior to yours.

How do you develop this mental attitude? Many sceptics see themselves as 'outsiders'. More than a few of the fund managers and other investors I researched and talked to in the course of writing this book had either spent time moving around as children or had in some other way felt slightly detached from their peer group. And if you think about the archetypal investment contrarians out there, they tend either to fall into the angry young man stereotype (hedge fund managers) or the worldly-wise old man, tutting at the folly of the world, stereotype (Warren Buffett and Howard Marks, for example). Sometimes this is just a pose, and sometimes it's just an excuse to be argumentative, and you certainly don't have to be a friendless outcast or the pub bore to be a sceptical investor. But you do have to have confidence in your own analysis and the ability to take the opinions of others with a big pinch of salt. As Mauboussin puts it: "Many successful investors have a skill that is very valuable in investing, but not so valuable for life: a blatant disregard for the views of others."

Of course, one way to get around all of this is simply not to share your opinions with others. You're not a hedge fund manager trying to drum up business, and you're not a talking head on CNBC. You're a private investor. Be private. Being right when everyone else is wrong is not the goal. Making money is the goal. As long as you do that, you've succeeded. The other market participants need not know that you achieved it by betting in the opposite direction to them.

3. DON'T BUY STORIES,
BUY FACTS

As we discussed earlier, we're suckers for stories, and the people who sell stocks and sell funds and sell 'ideas' all know that. That's why so many tech funds launched almost exactly as the tech bubble was about to burst in 2000, and it's why every time a new exchange-traded fund specialising in one sector or theme or strategy is launched, that particular sector tends to start wilting. The best time to sell a story is when the story is already popular. And that's the worst time to buy an investment. As James Montier (also of GMO) puts it, "the world would be a very dull place if we didn't have stories, it's the way people think. Unfortunately, it's not a great way to think about investing."

And if you think seasoned investors can't fall for a good story, just look at the cautionary tale of blood-testing start-up Theranos. All it took was a photogenic young female founder with an exciting 'disruptor' story to attract some of Silicon Valley's smartest venture capitalists to invest in the company. This was all despite the fact that Theranos was founded on an unproven 'magic blood-test' technology that no one bothered to investigate until an enterprising journalist, John Carreyrou, started posing awkward questions and paying attention to all the sceptical scientists who were asking why none of the science backing the tests had been peer-reviewed. It turned out that the company was an astounding triumph of hype and hope over scientific reality. The founder and CEO Elizabeth Holmes went from having an estimated value of $4.5bn in 2015, to $0 in 2016.

So do your research. All of the good stuff is in the details, because the details are where no one else bothers to look. And you don't have to do much to be better informed than the typical investor. *Wall Street Journal* columnist and author Jason Zweig recently highlighted a study which revealed that the average US company's annual report is only downloaded 29 times on its day of release. Even General Electric – one of America's biggest, most iconic companies – says that its annual report was only downloaded 800 times in 2013. In other words, a handful of people – in a world stuffed full of analysts and investors – are actually reading the most important public document that these companies release each year. So don't listen to stories – check the data out for yourself.

4. KNOW YOUR HISTORY

Our collective ability to imagine that we exist at some unique moment in history, in the face of all evidence to the contrary, is quite staggering. For example, the question: 'What if there was a run on a British bank?' didn't seriously occur to just about any investor before September 2007 and the run on Northern Rock. In the aftermath, there was a sense of shock, paralysis and disbelief. There's no doubt that it was a startling occurrence. But equally, banking crises have been regular occurrences in the past 100 years, across every country in the world, from Scandinavia in the 1990s to the US savings and loan crisis in the early 1980s.

The same went for just about every other aspect of the financial crisis. When quantitative easing (money printing by central banks) first arrived on the scene, almost everyone seemed to think that it was new, bar a few half-hearted efforts in Japan. But the Federal Reserve had in fact done it before, in very similar circumstances, after the Great Depression. Here's another example: all throughout the slow and painful recovery from the 2008 financial crisis, commentators have been talking of a "new normal" and "secular stagnation", and pondering over the length of time it has taken to bounce back, as though it's a mystery. And yet, economists Carmen Reinhart and Kenneth Rogoff published a high-profile book – *This Time Is Different* – about this very topic in 2009, just after the financial crisis started. They examined systemic banking crises across the world and concluded that the aftermath of such a crisis involved a prolonged period of extremely slow growth – it typically takes ten years for GDP per head to return to its pre-crisis peak, as opposed to a year or two for a 'normal' recession. In other words, there is nothing unique here – we have simply been enduring a typical post-banking-crisis recovery. Many high-profile, respected financial writers and economics professors are still asking: 'Why isn't this crisis over yet? What are we doing wrong?' and the simple answer, looking at history, is that these crises always take this long to fall out of the system. The only thing we're doing wrong is lacking the patience to wait.

This is not an argument that 'it's never different this time'. There are always significant factors that make each and every golden era or crisis period different from the rest. But very often, what's deemed 'unthinkable' and 'unprecedented' in the heat of the moment has in fact happened in a very similar manner in the surprisingly recent past. As Sir John Templeton put it (emphasis mine): "The investor who says, 'This time is different,' **when in fact it's virtually a repeat of an earlier situation**, has uttered among the four most costly words in the annals of investing." Developing a knowledge of and an appreciation for financial history will help you to understand just how rapidly things can change. This will give you the confidence to challenge the prevailing wisdom of the day (which almost always extrapolates itself into the far future), and to have a better idea of how to react when things do change.

Don't take my word for it. Ray Dalio is the founder of the world's biggest hedge fund business, Bridgewater Associates. He's one of the world's richest men and one of the most influential in finance. He also had a very painful learning experience on the value of knowing your history early on in his career. In 1982, Dalio was convinced that Mexico was set to default on its debts. Many of those loans were owed to US banks, and Dalio was convinced that the US market would collapse as a result. It was a controversial view at the time, but in August that year, when Mexico defaulted – as he'd predicted – it looked like a great contrarian call. Trouble was, while he was correct on Mexico going bust, the effect was the polar opposite of what he had anticipated. One problem was that US stock markets were already dirt cheap by this point, so all the bad news and more was already priced in. So rather than crashing, the market soared as the Federal Reserve stepped in to save the day, providing Mexico with short-term debt relief and slashing interest rates. Indeed, as financial historian Russell Napier points out, 1982 turned out to be one of the single most profitable years in the entire 20th century to buy stocks. Dalio meanwhile had to lay off all of the staff from his fledgling hedge fund. "I was so broke, I had to borrow $4,000 from my dad."

In an interview with lifestyle author Tim Ferriss, Dalio notes that this taught him the value of carefully studying the past. "One of the things I've learned over the years is that many surprises come because things that happen as surprises never happened in one's lifetime before. So it's advantageous to look beyond one's lifetime or beyond one's own experiences to understand how the world works so that one can anticipate all of those things … Almost everything happens over and over again through history … the key to success is to identify what one of those [examples is most relevant] … If you're not dealing with it that way, then everything is a one-off."

There's another key contrarian trait that a good grasp of financial history can help you to build: patience. One of the biggest challenges you'll face as a sceptical investor is that it inevitably involves being wrong for at least a short period of time (and often longer). If you're betting against the market, then by definition the market won't go your way in the early stages of that bet. You will constantly be questioning yourself and your assumptions. This is useful to an extent (and we'll look at this more in chapter 9), but there's a fine line between healthy self-doubt and a damaging lack of conviction. As Howard Marks puts it: "In order to be a superior investor, you need the strength to diverge from the herd, stand by your convictions, and maintain positions until events prove them right." Having a solid understanding of how markets have evolved in the past will help you to recognise the truth of the old saying, 'this too shall pass'.

CHAPTER

6

Beating Your Brain – Process Versus Outcome

WHEN I WAS studying psychology at university back in the 1990s, one book in particular caught my imagination, principally because it was short and I was lazy. It's called *Three Psychologies: Perspectives from Freud, Skinner and Rogers* by Robert D. Nye, and I'd highly recommend it. It's an excellent bluffer's guide to some of the most important theories in psychology. It takes Sigmund Freud, Carl Rogers and B. F. Skinner, and looks at their own individual models of the world (broadly speaking, one pessimistic, one optimistic and one neutral), how they explained human behaviour, and their influence on our understanding of personality.

Freud was great at describing our inner world, with a poetic, if fatalistic, view of human nature. His idea that our conscious mind (the 'ego') is the product of a raging war between our instincts (the 'id') and our conscience and society's expectations (the 'superego') is elegant and evocative. But he wasn't great at explaining how to reconcile this turbulent, Jekyll-and-Hyde netherworld with the mundane demands of everyday life.

Rogers had a far more optimistic view of human nature, which by temperament appealed to me more. His view was that progress, fulfilment and happiness – "self-actualisation" – were possible, and that, once our basic physical needs are met, we all just want to be loved and accepted and given the opportunity to become the best version of ourselves that we can be. But his theory lacked Freud's compelling darkness, and it also inspired a lot of the flakier type of self-help book.

The driest of the three was Burrhus Frederic Skinner (more frequently known as B. F. Skinner). But as I've got older, he's also the one I have the most time for. Skinner believed that our behaviour was largely dictated by our environment, and our experiences of interacting with the world. Put simply, Skinner didn't see us as being much different to trained animals – positive reinforcement (good things happening) would make us repeat an action. Negative reinforcement (bad things happening) would put us off doing something. On the face of it, it's a heartless, reductive view of humanity. Both the passion of Freud and the optimism of Rogers are more inspiring. And Skinner's theory was undoubtedly over-simplistic – like most of us, he saw his own world view as an all-encompassing 'theory of everything' rather than a clever model with a wide range of useful applications. He placed too much importance on learned behaviour and the external environment, and not enough on genetic differences and our interior world (in the 'nature vs nurture' debate, he's very much on the side of 'nurture').

However, Skinner's great strength is that his theory lends itself to practical solutions to cognitive problems. Present a psychological problem to Freud, and he'd have you lie on the couch, raking over some repressed childhood trauma over and over again, until you reached 'catharsis' and your troubles miraculously vanished. Skinner was more interested in how to alter an individual's environment in order to change their behaviour, and thus make their life easier. Take one minor example from his own life: as with many of us, Skinner found that as he got older he often forgot to take his umbrella outdoors with him, even if the weather forecast was predicting showers later that day. So he simply trained himself to hang his umbrella on the door handle as soon as he heard a forecast for rain. He didn't spend lots of time worrying about the cause – he just found a solution.

Why does all of this matter? Because while resisting the desire to run with the crowd is a big part of being a successful sceptical investor, it's not sufficient by itself. You also need to avoid falling prey to the tripwires in your own mind, of which there are plenty. So in this chapter we'll delve into many of the psychological quirks that make human beings entirely unsuited to the world of investment. But rather than spend too much time agonising about why this is, I want to focus on how you can tame your brain and control your environment – and help your mind to work with you, rather than against you.

Here are just a few ways in which your brain sabotages your investments

As we discussed in chapter 5, the expansionary and contractionary instincts are constantly interfering with your thought processes. Both inspire panic – a desire to take evasive action of one sort or another and make rapid, gut-level decisions. These instincts have evolved with good reason, but they are entirely self-defeating when it comes to making considered choices in an investment environment which is constantly pushing your buttons. And make no mistake, it does push your buttons. As Jason Zweig points out in his book, *Your Money and Your Brain* (2007), "financial losses are processed in the same areas of the brain that respond to mortal danger", while "the neural activity of someone whose investments are making money is indistinguishable from that of someone who is high on cocaine". In short, when it comes to investing, you are not nearly as in control as you might imagine you are. Here's a by-no-means-comprehensive rundown of some of your brain's worst tendencies when confronted with making choices about money.

YOU ARE TERRIBLE AT JUDGING WHAT'S RELEVANT

Faced with a decision that involves uncertainty – such as investing – your brain will attempt to speed up the process by seeking out any information it can to feed into that process. The problem is, it will do this regardless of whether the information is actually helpful or not. In the case of 'anchoring', Amos Tversky and Daniel Kahneman – two of the best-known behavioural economists – found that even an entirely irrelevant piece of information can be harnessed as a reference point by individuals trying to make an estimate about an unknown quantity. In a famous 1974 paper ('Judgement under uncertainty: heuristics and biases'), the pair detailed an experiment in which they had asked a group of subjects to make estimates of unfamiliar quantities. Before they did so, they spun a wheel to produce a random number between 0 and 100. The subject was asked a question, along the lines of: 'Is the percentage of African countries in the United Nations higher or lower than this number?' They would then be asked to give their exact estimate. The higher the number on the wheel, the higher the estimates; the lower the number, the lower the estimates. In other words, the subjects used the random number as a mental 'anchor' – even though it was obviously entirely irrelevant.

This doesn't just apply to numbers. Robert Shiller, for example, talks about how hearing bad news stories (those with "negative emotional valence") about, say, natural disasters, increases people's estimates of the likelihood of a stock market crash, even though the incidence of earthquakes (for example) has no impact on or information value for forecasting the direction of financial markets.

A similar example is the prevalence of the 'availability heuristic' – this is our tendency, as Kahneman puts it, "to judge the probability of an event by the ease with which we can call it to mind". Clearly what is memorable and what is likely are two different things – it's much easier to remember significant incidents, or events that have just happened ('recency bias') and overestimate the chances of them happening again in the near future, compared to their historic frequency. An obvious example is the fact that people grow warier of investing in stocks in the aftermath of a market crash, whereas history shows that this is precisely when we should be getting excited about buying.

Another factor that plays havoc with our ability to make good decisions is the power of 'framing' – whereby individuals can be swayed into making different choices based on how data is presented, rather than its content. For example, when asked about hypothetical medical interventions, more people will favour an intervention if the choice is presented in terms of lives saved, rather than if the odds of death are highlighted instead – even if the information is the same in both instances.

YOU ARE TOO HIGHLY EVOLVED
FOR YOUR OWN GOOD

As we noted in chapter 5, our pattern-spotting addiction is useful for figuring out how things work, but in certain situations it is self-destructive – in fact, the average pigeon might well be better equipped for investing than you are. How do we know that? In one type of experiment, researchers flash a green or red light onto a screen, and the subject's job is to predict which light will flash on next (when the subject is a pigeon – or a rat – rather than a human, they are trained to do the task by receiving a reward when they press the right button). The lights appear in a random order, but unbeknown to the subject, on 80% of occasions, it's the green light and on 20% of occasions it's the red light. Clearly, the best strategy is to go for green every time – that way you'll win 80% of the time. And before too long, rats and pigeons figure this out – it's random, but green obviously comes up a lot more than red, so you might as well always go for green and get a treat most of the time.

But humans can't get to grips with this. We want to find a pattern that will enable us to get 100% of the treats, and we are convinced that we can do it. So while most human subjects rapidly grasp that green is coming up roughly four in five times, they still don't go for the optimum strategy of picking green every time. Instead, they'll press green roughly 80% of the time, but then opt for red every so often, believing that they can predict when it'll next come up. As a result, their hit rate ends up being below 80%. What's even more striking is that humans persist in trying to beat the system, even when they've been told by the experimenter that the order of the lights flashing is random. We continue to demand and expect order where there is no order to be found.

YOU ARE PRIMED TO FEAR LOSSES MORE THAN YOU VALUE GAINS...

You hate losing more than you love winning. In fact, research has shown that the pain of a loss is roughly twice as acute as the pleasure from a gain. There are good evolutionary reasons for this – a loss might kill you, a gain will just make your current situation better – but again, it's not helpful in terms of how you think about investing.

Having a focus on the downside is a healthy thing in investment, so this might not seem to be a problem – but annoyingly, it's not as simple as that. You see, when you are sitting on a loss (which is bound to happen at some point), you don't want to crystallise it, and as a result, you will run ever-greater risks to avoid it, or to claw the money back. As behavioural economist Andrew Lo, author of *Adaptive Markets*, pointed out in a 2015 paper on emotions and investment, this is often at the heart of rogue trader scandals – Nick Leeson brought down Barings Bank in 1995 by effectively playing double or quits with a bad bet on Japanese stocks and constantly covering it up in an effort to recoup his earlier losses.

...AND YET YOU ARE HOPELESSLY OVER-OPTIMISTIC AND HUNGRY FOR GAINS

There's a wonderful retelling of the Pandora myth, in which 'hope' is not the consolation prize, but the last and most evil creature to fly out of the box of horrors. In this version, hope is what keeps us striving in the face of pain and futility, subjecting ourselves to ever more punishment, even though we are ultimately doomed to fail. This is a somewhat grim view of life and not one I'd echo, but when it comes to investing, this isn't a bad way to think about hope. Hope will drag you into making investment mistakes, because hope presents you with dreams of the big gains, and hope – regardless of how much you make – is never satisfied. This is because, as Zweig points out, the part of your brain that gets excited by investment gains is stimulated more by the expectation – the hope – of gains than the actual getting of those gains. "It's expectation – not satiation – that causes arousal," notes Zweig. Again, this is another evolutionary tripwire – the hope of making a gain motivates you to get out there and take the risk of getting it. That's fine when your life depends on expanding your environmental comfort zone – your Stone Age ancestors' peers, who were instead constantly paralysed by fear of the downside, presumably stayed in their caves and starved themselves out of the evolutionary race – but it's not ideal when the desire to take a risk in this context can be indulged by merely pressing a few buttons on a laptop.

YOU THINK YOU'RE ALWAYS RIGHT EVEN WHEN YOU'RE DEFINITELY WRONG

As we discussed in chapter 5 (and will revisit in chapter 9) we hate inconsistencies in our world view, but rather than confront them and amend our world view correspondingly, we're happier to sweep them under the carpet or, better yet, never encounter them at all. When it comes to investing, this manifests itself in a tendency to deceive ourselves about our investing prowess – almost every investor believes that they are better than average, even though that's clearly mathematically impossible. 'Hindsight bias' – whereby we justify a decision by pretending that we knew the outcome was inevitable – is just one example of the self-delusion that this encourages. It doesn't help that we also suffer from the 'endowment effect'. This is the tendency to value an asset or object that we already own more highly than one that we don't – even if they are both exactly the same.

To sum up, you are designed to be a bad investor. You are terrible at weighing up the importance of different pieces of information, or even figuring out which information is relevant. You panic when things go wrong, which leads you to sell your winners too early, and to chase losses. You don't just hold on to your losers, you take bigger risks to compensate for those losses, digging an even deeper hole for yourself in the process. Despite all this, you have too much faith in your own ability.

And this is just the tip of the iceberg. There are plenty of other cognitive biases and tripwires in your brain – too many to run through here. But the nastiest thing about these traps is this: the fact that you are aware of them makes very little difference to your ability to surmount them. There's a great story related by Michael Batnick of the Irrelevant Investor blog, about billionaire Stanley Druckenmiller. Druckenmiller is one of the most successful and highly respected active investors around today. Yet during the tech bubble of the late 1990s, he succumbed to fear of losing out, piling into technology stocks at the very peak. He lost a fortune – "I bought $6bn worth of tech stocks and in six weeks I had lost $3bn in that one play," he told an interviewer in 2015. When asked what he had learned from the error, he replied: "I didn't learn anything. I already knew that I wasn't supposed to do that. I was just an emotional basket case and I couldn't help myself."

So you can be very aware of all of your psychological flaws as an investor. It makes no difference – when you're in the thick of it, your instincts will take over, like a runaway horse, leaving you frantically clinging to the reins even as your path takes you over a cliff.

To be a better investor you need to make better decisions

Being a better investor is about making better decisions. Every investment is a bet on the future. You cannot know the future and you cannot control it. The key to investing well is to make good decisions in the face of that uncertainty, based on a strong understanding of your goals and a strong understanding of the tools available to help you to achieve those goals. A single good decision may lead to a bad outcome. And a single bad decision may result in a good outcome. But the making of many good decisions, over time, should compound into a better outcome than the making of a series of bad decisions. You can't legislate for the impact of luck, but people who consistently make good decisions tend to get luckier than those who repeatedly make bad ones.

Making good investment decisions is a challenge – but it is not a life-or-death situation. The problem is, your brain treats it that way. So what can you do? The good news is that, with effort, you can sidestep your brain's worst habits. In his bestseller, *Thinking, Fast and Slow*, Daniel Kahneman distinguishes between System 1 thinking, which is fast and instinctive, and System 2, which is more deliberate and logical. Most cognitive biases arise from System 1 – thinking with your gut, basically. That works fine in some cases – your gut is helpful in many situations – but not for investing. So how can we be sure to use System 2 instead and make considered, rational decisions based on facts rather than cognitive shortcuts?

Making good decisions is mostly about putting distance between your 'gut' and your investment choices. You can't control the outcome of your investment decisions. But you *can* control the process by which you come to those decisions, and you can control the environment in which you make them. That's the best way to get System 2 working for you.

CULTIVATE GOOD INVESTMENT HABITS BY WORKING IN A HEALTHY ENVIRONMENT

"In theory, there is no difference between theory and practice. In practice, there is." This popular quote is attributed to various wits, but regardless of who said it, it sums up one of the major paradoxes of investing. You can 'know' how things should work, but in the thick of it, it's easy to abandon all of your principles. So you need to create an investment process that prevents you from making big behavioural errors in practice, even if — in theory — that means embracing some inefficiencies along the way. That involves understanding your own particular weak spots and making sure that you create an investment environment that works for you, rather than against you.

For example, we all know how exciting investment can feel — you read a hot tip and you immediately want to grab your phone and press 'buy'. Stop. You shouldn't even have an app like that on your phone. Delete it. It makes impulsive action too easy. Before you buy or sell anything, you should be forced to sit at your desk, make a conscious decision to open your broker's website, and fill in your password and the rest of it (don't let Google save the details for you), before you can act on the trade. To prevent the impulsive System 1 process from taking over, you have to slow down – so put up obstacles to taking rapid action.

Similarly, avoid consuming the news unconsciously, because it will influence your emotional state. You should read selectively and in a deliberate manner for research (we'll look in more detail at how to use the media in the next chapter), but don't have Twitter open on your desktop churning out investment views, or a financial news TV station blaring in the background somewhere, or busy screens full of flashing tickers and fluctuating charts cluttering up your psychological landscape.

On that note, it also makes sense to do your research when the market is closed, so that you are not tempted to act on an impulse to buy before you've had time to finish your research and to reflect on it. After all, if you are planning to hold this asset for any reasonable length of time (and remember that patience is a critical personality trait for a sceptical investor) then you should be happy to put aside the hours it takes to do your homework first. So do your research, write out a plan, and only then should you open your account and act on that plan.

Ultimately, this is very simple stuff – it's the same as trying to avoid any other form of bad behaviour. If you want to cut down on booze, avoid going to the pub or the off-licence. If you want to cut down on the morning cappuccino, take a different route to work. If you want to stop smoking, start having conversations with your office gossip mate in the kitchen rather than at the fire exit. It's hard enough to resist your destructive urges – the least you can do for yourself is to make your environment more supportive of your best intentions.

ALWAYS FOCUS ON THE DOWNSIDE

"Rule number one: don't lose money. Rule number two: remember rule number one." This may be Warren Buffett's most infuriatingly oblique piece of investment advice (and he's got a few). Every investment requires you to take the risk of losing money. If you knew how to avoid losing money, you wouldn't have to read books like this one because you'd just stick your money in the market and it'd go up. But really Buffett is just over-exaggerating to emphasise an extremely important point – when you're investing you should always focus on the downside, the worst-case scenario. What could go wrong? How badly would it hurt?

I know what you're thinking – 'if we suffer from loss aversion, then isn't this a bad thing?' But the annoying thing about loss aversion is that it only kicks in at the worst possible time – when you're actually losing money, and you have no plan, and you're wildly panicking about what to do. That's when you make the mistakes and start desperately flailing around taking extra risks to try to win back your losses.

Before you go into an investment, loss aversion isn't the issue – because you don't expect to make a loss. You're excited about the investment, because you know it's going to go well. It's all unicorns and multibaggers and never having to work again. The idea of losing money isn't even on the table, because you always do your homework and you're always right.

So Buffett – for all of his gratingly folksy manner – is correct in forcefully making the point that you need to focus on losing money, because every instinct in your brain would rather focus on making money. System 1 thinks about the upside, piles in, then throws a screaming hissy fit when things don't go your way. Thinking about the downside might be a lot less fun, but it means that you'll allow System 2 to kick in and plan the investment sensibly, and in doing so, stay solvent and sane, rather than dreaming futilely of getting rich quick.

HAVE AN AUTO-PILOT WORKING FOR YOU

Another good way to get System 2 working for you is to take as many decisions as possible in advance. One way to do that is to put a stop-loss in place (a share price at which you will sell) when you invest. As the Enterprising Investor blogger on the CFA Institute website points out, although there's no evidence that stop-losses systematically improve returns, they can help to instil discipline. For a start, it forces you to consider the worst-case scenario before you invest – encouraging that all-important focus on the downside. It also gives you an explicit point at which you are forced to re-evaluate a stock (after it's been sold) without being influenced by the aforementioned endowment effect. You can adjust your use of stop-losses to taste, your own investment style, and the specific nature of the investment (you want to set the stop-loss at a sufficient distance to avoid being shaken out of the position by bog-standard volatility – so you'd have a wider stop-loss on an AIM stock than on a FTSE 100 stalwart, for example). But if you are going to use stop-losses then I'd be inclined to use a 'hard' stop, where your broker automatically sells at a preset point. The alternative is to use a 'soft' stop-loss, where you make a mental note to sell if a share falls to a certain price, but it takes incredible discipline to stick to that – more often than not you'll fall prey to hindsight bias and you'll rewrite history so as to find a reason as to why this particular fall is an 'exception' and thus justify breaking your own rule in the process.

KEEP A DIARY

Before you enter an investment, you have to have a plan – both for what happens if your investment goes wrong, and for what happens if it goes right. And you also have to be able to review the results of your process as neutrally as possible, so that you can see what's working and what isn't. A simple, practical solution to both of these problems is to keep an investment journal.

This journal can be digital or written, whatever you prefer – some would argue that the act of physically writing forces you to make more considered decisions, but I'd say that it's more important to do something that you'll stick to. Before you invest, you should record the details of what you plan to invest in, and the price at which you are investing. But you should also explain your exact rationale for investing, and under what circumstances you would either take profits, or sell at a loss.

This will slow down your investment process and enable System 2 to kick in, but crucially it also means that you have a record of your thought processes that you can review at a later date. This is vital if you want to hold yourself to account. Again, hindsight bias and your ego's other defence mechanisms are astoundingly powerful. Without keeping a proper track record, you will remember your triumphs and ignore your failures, to the point where you might be losing money but still regard yourself as a great investor because of that one time that you managed to double your money after taking a punt on a junior mining stock. Writing it down will keep you honest.

Your investment journal doesn't have to take a specific format – it's something you can customise to suit your own investment style. However, the key thing to remember is to write in it *before* you invest, not afterwards. The whole point of doing this is to slow yourself down and give System 2 a chance to kick in. It's a fact-finding mission as much as anything else – it's about making sure that you have a sufficient understanding of what you are buying before you invest in it, and also making sure that you have a plan for what to do if things go wrong. It'll also prevent you from overtrading, which means you don't lose as much money on costs.

So what should go in your diary? You can customise your own investment journal. But here are the sorts of things I would record in it:

- **The basics:** write down the date; what you're buying; the estimated all-in transaction costs (what'll it cost you to buy, hold, and sell); the purchase price; the date of the next dividend payout (if applicable); the expected payout; and the dividend yield on the purchase price. Then, when you close the trade, you'll want to add the date you exited; the exit price; the confirmed all-in costs; and the total return (i.e. including dividends or interest income, and subtracting costs).

- **Source of idea:** what made you want to investigate this investment further? Where did you get the idea from? You may find that some sources are better than others. Or that some pundits are fantastic contrarian indicators and others are not.

- **Your rationale for buying:** markets are priced based on expectations. As a sceptical investor, you are trying to exploit the gap between the market's expectations for how things will turn out (the current price) and your own belief of how things will turn out. So why are you right? And why is the market wrong? Trying to articulate this in writing will rapidly expose any gaps in your knowledge or flaws in your logic.

- **What return do you hope to make, and over what sort of time frame?** The level of specificity here will vary depending on the time frame and your investment style. You may have a rough percentage in mind over a very long period of time, or you might have a quite specific target price. The point is to have an idea of how you expect the investment to perform so that when you come to review the idea in the future, you can see what actually happened – where you went wrong, and what you got right.

- **What would make you sell?** Think about how far the price would have to fall before you reconsidered your rationale for buying. In effect, what price would prove you wrong? And what will you do if it ends up there? (There may be other reasons to sell too – your rationale for buying may be proved wrong well before the price falls to your selling point – but this is a good exercise in preparing yourself for the worst-case scenario, rather than panicking when it happens.)

- **What's your emotional state?** How do you feel? You don't have to make this detailed – one word would do. Calm is good. Almost everything else is bad. Angry (watch out). Drunk (not good). Tired (think twice). I'm not saying that this should prevent you from doing anything. But it's worth keeping a note of these because it's useful to look back and see if certain states of mind are more or less conducive to making good trades.

- **What could I invest in instead?** You aren't a fund manager. You don't need a benchmark. But you do need to be aware of risk. And being keenly aware of what you could have invested in instead will help you to remain disciplined. So if you are buying an individual stock, ask yourself this: why are you investing in this stock, instead of in an exchange-traded fund (ETF) or tracker that would cover the whole stock market and give you a lot more diversification in the process? And make it a benchmark that forces you to ask yourself tough questions. For example, if you decide to buy an individual big mining stock – BHP Billiton, say – then an obvious comparator to use is the FTSE 100. But then it's easy to say: 'I'm buying BHP instead of the wider index because I want exposure to the mining sector, which I believe will outperform, and I don't want all the other rubbish that comes with the FTSE 100.' A better benchmark in this case would be the FTSE Mining Sector, or a mining sector investment trust. Then the question becomes: why are you taking the risk of buying this particular mining stock, rather than a mining fund? What's special about this one? This will force you to analyse the idea behind your trade further. Do you really want to buy BHP? Or do you just want to buy miners? And if it's the latter, then despite BHP's position as a mining major, you'd still be better off risk-wise by buying a fund. A huge part of successful investing is executing well on a good idea, and thinking about this will help you to understand whether you are using the correct financial instrument to turn your good contrarian idea into an efficiently executed investment.

USING YOUR JOURNAL

Review your positions regularly. Don't just revisit investments that go down or ones that you've sold – revisit the ones that go up too. Is your rationale for buying still valid? Update your view, and if necessary update your targets. It can also be worth continuing to follow investments that you have sold out of. You have to be careful with this – you don't want to fall prey to Jim Bowen Syndrome (Bowen was the presenter of 1980s gameshow *Bullseye*, who gleefully revealed to contestants the prizes they'd missed out on with the words: "Here's what you could have won"). And you certainly don't want to end up feeling as though your 30% gain is in fact a huge loss because it carried on rising to 50%. But if you are persistently making similar errors – selling out of a stock that then rapidly recovers (perhaps your stop-losses are too tight for the type of stock you are buying?) or taking profits far too early (perhaps because you are too concerned about those profits turning into losses?), then it might be worth revisiting your strategy and tweaking it accordingly.

You may question the hassle of doing this, but I think it's essential. If you don't keep records of your investment decision process (as well as your investment results) then you won't be able to judge if you're getting any better. Investing can be an enjoyable pasttime – an excuse for reading about topics you're interested in, and giving your mental muscles a workout – and that's all good.

But regardless of how much you enjoy it, you don't want to get to retirement and realise that you could have kept the lot in a 60/40 equity/bond portfolio and made more money while avoiding all that work. So if you've decided that you want to try to beat the market, then you have to strive to get better – and the only way to do that is to keep a record of your performance.

CHAPTER

7

How to Use the Media

I REMEMBER VERY clearly the first inkling I had that we must be reaching a turning point in the great financial crisis. It was January 2009 (29 January to be precise). It's fading into the mists of memory now, but it really is hard to exaggerate the sheer level of fear and urgency that was in the air at this point. The banking system was in an extremely precarious state. Our most-read articles at *MoneyWeek* were consistently those that analysed the solvency of the banks that were still standing. It may be the only period in history during which the mildly informed man or woman in the street knew exactly which high street banks had the worst CDS spreads, what that meant, and why it mattered.

Anyway, I was rushing off to work, looking forward to a day of picking through the financial debris to work out what was going to go pear-shaped next. I went to pick up a morning paper. Most were leading on financial stories, as you'd expect, but I remember that on the paper racks, one front page really stood out – the *Times*. It was a single story front page. The headline read: 'The worst recession'. The story itself was unremarkable – an anodyne piece on a gloomy report that had just been released by the International Monetary Fund (IMF) on the state of the global economy.

What struck me was the picture they'd chosen to illustrate it. It was an image of St Paul's Cathedral during the Blitz. Combined with the stark, single-sentence headline, and the single story dominating the front page, the overall impression was one of extraordinary panic. It seemed to be saying: 'This is as bad as the Blitz. This is an existential crisis. Take cover now.' And that, of course, was a gross exaggeration. The financial crisis had been a massive shock and central bankers and politicians were still wrapping their heads around how to deal with it. Fears that cash machines would dry up and that civil disorder would result were at the forefront of everyone's minds. But it wasn't – by any stretch of the imagination – the second world war. The people I was rushing to work with might be living in fear for their jobs, but we could be pretty confident that our places of work would still be standing by the end of the day.

At that point, despite my bearish inclination, and my strong belief that worse was to come due to the knock-on effects of bank lending drying up and further holes being found in balance sheets everywhere, I did start to think: 'OK, we've now moved into the "melodrama" phase of the crisis. People are about as scared as they can get.' And when people are as scared as they can get, the only way is up – things can still be bad, but even a move from 'screaming panic' to 'scared stiff' is an improvement.

It wasn't the precise bottom of the market by any means. That day, the FTSE 100 closed at 4190. It was just over another month before it hit its crisis low of 3512 on 3 March. However, within another two months – by 30 April, to be precise – the FTSE 100 was back above 4190. So if you'd bought in – or at least started drip-feeding money in on a regular basis – on the day that you'd read that particular front page, you'd have certainly required nerves of steel, as the market fell by a further 700 points – not far off 20%. But you'd have been back to even within three months, and – other than a few hairy moments in July – you'd have remained above water for the rest of the subsequent bull market. Not only that, but you'd have the bragging rights to being able to say that you'd bought pretty near the bottom of the biggest bear market in a generation. Not a bad position to be in.

The magazine cover indicator

The *Times* headline is an example of a well-known contrarian investment signal known as the 'magazine cover indicator'. Fundamentally, investment is all about the flow of money. An old City joke goes: 'Why did the market go up today? More buyers than sellers.' The magazine cover indicator is the idea that, by the time an investment story has become so popular that it can hit the front page of a major media publication – newspapers or magazines mainly, although clearly the internet is now muddying the water somewhat – then its days as a profitable idea must be numbered. Everyone who is interested in the story has almost certainly already bought into it, so there can be very few potential buyers (or sellers, if it's a negative story) left, which in turn suggests that the flow of money is about to reverse. In short, as financial writer and former fund manager Jonathan Compton has often said to me: "If it's in the press, it's in the price."

The indicator originates with US financial analyst, writer and investment manager Paul Macrae Montgomery, who came up with the idea in the early 1980s. He looked at *Time* magazine covers going back to the 1920s. He found that in general, when the cover was bullish on the stock market, you could make good profits by buying and holding for the next 30 days. However, at that point, you had better sell out – for the subsequent 11 months, returns were negative. The same held true in reverse for bearish covers – sell short for 30 days, then go long for the rest of the year. In other words, *Time* magazine tended to anticipate a turning point in the market by about a month. Montgomery's theory didn't just apply to *Time* magazine, but it had three basic rules. Firstly, the publication in question had to be a mainstream magazine, not one whose primary focus was business (although the reality is that business mags can be pretty good indicators too, as we'll see a bit later). Secondly, the cover story had to deal with a "well-understood concept that is reaching a climax". Finally, there had to have been significant gains leading up to the cover being published. So, for Montgomery, this was very much about finding the turning point in an already overexposed story.

The more aggressive the cover, the more drastic the subsequent turn. As contrarian investment manager Ned Davis notes in his book *The Triumph of Contrarian Investing*, "between 1966 and 1982, the Dow Jones Industrial Average saw five rallies and four declines of greater than 30%. At or near many of those peaks and troughs were cover stories that, in hindsight, would have been good contrary indicators." One impressive example, notes Davis, was the cover of *Newsweek* on 9 September 1974. The story came in the depths of the global stock market crash of the early 1970s. The Dow Jones index had collapsed to 600-odds, from a peak of around 1050 in early January 1973, and investors were badly shaken. The cover depicted an angry bear tearing down the pillars of the stock market, Samson-and-Delilah style. The headline, plastered in white on red across the top, was 'The Big Bad Bear'. The market continued lower into October, rebounded sharply in early November, and then hit a final bear market low of 577 in early December 1974. Once again, if you'd started investing when that September cover story came out, you'd have got in just three months before the ultimate end of a painful two-year bear market. And within less than a year, you'd have made a very healthy return indeed – by mid-1975, the market was back up challenging the 900 mark.

The proof is in the publishing

Although reading the media is as much art as science, plenty of studies since have backed up Montgomery's broad thesis. One of the most recent examples was a study by Greg Marks and Brent Donnelly at Citibank, which focused on the *Economist*. The pair looked at every cover story from the current affairs and news weekly going back to 1998. They selected those stories that covered "an emotional or hyperbolic portrayal of an asset class or market-related theme". They looked for covers that made clear reference to "a market theme or asset class"; made a strong statement – bullish or bearish – on said asset class; and where an obvious contrarian trade was available. In all, they found 44 such covers, and then tracked the given asset class's performance over the next three, six and 12 months. What did they find? The results "strongly suggest that covers from the *Economist* are a reverse indicator." Within six to 12 months, nearly 70% of the covers ("a very high success rate") had proven to be good contrarian indicators – in other words, you could make money by doing the opposite of what the cover indicated.

One infamous example came in early March 1999. The *Economist* published a cover story with a picture of two roughnecks wrestling with a gushing oil well. The headline was 'Drowning in oil'. At the time, the oil price (as judged by the European benchmark, Brent crude) was sitting at a historical low of around $10 a barrel. Within a month, it was almost $15, and by March 2000, oil was trading at $30 a barrel. If you had placed a 'long' bet on the oil price on the day of publication, you would have spent virtually no time at all in the red. Indeed, the oil price has never again fallen as low as $10 a barrel at any point since that particular *Economist* cover was published.

A less-well-known sequel to this particular cover was published almost exactly ten years later. The international edition of *Newsweek* published a cover boasting the headline 'Cheap oil forever'. On publication in late April 2009, the price of oil was hovering around the $50-a-barrel mark, having dropped sharply following the financial crisis. Within a month, it was just under $60 a barrel; within a year, it was over $80; and it spent most of the subsequent three years ranging above $100 a barrel. Indeed, the oil price wouldn't see the $50 mark again from almost the moment that cover was published until another oil crash came in late 2014.

The indicator is by no means perfect, of course. Somewhat ironically, I think this is best demonstrated by one classic cover that's often cited as a great example of the power of the magazine cover indicator. The cover of the August 13 1979 issue of *Business Week* depicted a crumpled share certificate folded into a paper aeroplane that had nose-dived into the ground. The headline was: 'The death of equities'. It was certainly dramatic, and if you'd had the guts to buy then and hold for another ten years, you would have been very happy. But it hardly marked the bottom of the market. When the cover came out, the Dow Jones was sitting at not far off 870. It didn't actually bottom out until three years later in 1982, at around 780. So while it didn't fall a lot further, it did take its sweet time – and you'd have been biting your nails all the way along.

It's not just asset prices as a whole – it's individual stocks too

This is far from the only study to highlight the power of the cover story. In 2007, researchers from the University of Richmond Robins School of Business looked at 549 cover stories from *BusinessWeek*, *Forbes* and *Fortune*, spanning a period of around 20 years. In short, they found that covers that were positive on the featured company predicted poor subsequent stock performance, and the bad ones predicted improving performance. One of the main reasons for this turnaround is the timing of the covers – the companies that enjoyed positive coverage had on average beaten the market by more than 40% in the run-up to the front-page appearance. Meanwhile, the companies that suffered negative coverage had lagged the market by nearly 35% on average. In other words, the nature of the coverage reflected the prior performance of the stocks, rather than the future prospects. And, of course, by the time these stocks had reached the point where their stellar performance was being hailed on the front pages – or their woes were being picked over – it was all in the price. Investors were overly optimistic on the stars, and overly pessimistic on the also-rans. As a result, the disliked stocks went on to outperform the market by an average of just over 12%, but the most popular ones – while still outperforming – only beat the market by around 4%.

Another factor to be wary of is the celebrity CEO. As Barry Ritholtz points out, in December 1999, Amazon founder and CEO Jeff Bezos was picked as *Time* magazine's Person of the Year and graced the magazine's cover as a result. The tech bubble burst just three months later, in March 2000 (and Amazon's stock hit a high of $113 on 10 December 1999 – a level it would not see again until October 2009, nearly ten years later).

The media is a lot more than just newspapers

Of course, it's not just the newspapers that can reveal the prevailing sentiment of the day. Everything from popular TV shows to books to new product launches can indicate over-excitement or despondency. Again, it's all about how unusual or eye-catching the event happens to be. One of the most spectacular pieces of contrarian timing in recent history arose out of a US chat show. After the 2008 financial crisis had left the banks lurching from bust to bailout to congressional committee to half-hearted apologies or blank denials, there was understandably a great deal of public anger. After witnessing a pundit from business channel CNBC make a dismissive quip about how homeowners shouldn't be bailed out, Jon Stewart, host of *The Daily Show*, took an in-depth and critical look at the cheerleading tone of much of CNBC's financial market coverage prior to the crisis.

The coverage was particularly critical of Jim Cramer, the manic, generally bullish, host of share-tipping show, *Mad Money*, and one of the most identifiable faces of CNBC. Cramer agreed to go on *The Daily Show* in an attempt to defend himself. Instead, Stewart absolutely mauled him, broadcasting clip after clip where Cramer had talked about buying Bear Stearns or Lehman Brothers, and had downplayed the extent of the crisis. Both men still have good careers today, but it's quite the takedown (you can still watch it on YouTube). Cramer – not usually one to back down or be lost for words, and to be fair to him, certainly no worse than any other stock pundit – is left looking dazed and genuinely remorseful by the end of the beating. If there was ever a visual metaphor for America being sick to its heart of the financial sector and its shenanigans, it was that week of television.

It also marked the buying opportunity of the decade. *The Daily Show*'s series of CNBC takedowns kicked off on 4 March 2009. The S&P 500 hit its final bear market low on 9 March 2009. And the Stewart vs Cramer episode aired on 12 March. If you'd bought then – on the day that America's best-known stock promoter was being publicly pilloried by one of America's best-known comedians – you'd have made a fortune.

Another eye-catching move came in May 2007, when Condé Nast – one of the most powerful luxury magazine publishers in the world – decided to enter the dirty world of finance with the launch of its very first monthly wealth management title, Condé Nast Portfolio, just a few months before the credit crunch bit down hard. The title was understandably short-lived – magazines are expensive to produce at the best of times, and with advertising budgets among financial companies drying up fast, it was never going to last. However, it limped along for two years, and released its last issue in April 2009 – just in time for the market bottom.

Why does the magazine indicator work?

Think about mainstream film magazines (as opposed to arty, niche magazines). Who gets to be on most front covers? Famous people and big new releases? Or bit-part actors and independent films? Famous people, of course. It's the same for newspapers and current affairs magazines. The stories that make the front pages are the ones that are likely to have the highest emotional resonance with the audience of the newspaper or magazine – the stories that they care most about. The big stories.

A lot of people are suspicious of the media, which is understandable. Commercial newspapers and broadcasters are powerful institutions. Each of them – even those that strive to be neutral – has a political viewpoint that manifests itself in editorial decisions on which facts are reported and which commentators are quoted, and whose voices are loudest in any ensuing debate.

However, as a sceptical thinker, you need to understand that journalists do not 'manufacture' the news. There is no grand conspiracy – journalists certainly help to shape the stories that capture the public imagination, but by and large, they are chasing audience share, because without readers or viewers, these institutions cannot survive. So journalists report on what they (or their editors) think people most want to read. The more widely read the story, the bigger it gets, and the greater the readers' appetite for more, until it finally hits a peak. In other words, journalism is reflexive, just like the market.

So how does this translate to reporting on financial markets? When you're a journalist, you have to find reasons for things happening. If prices are high and rising, then explaining it by saying: 'this is happening because people are prone to over-enthusiasm and have a tendency to chase prices like dogs chase their tails', does not count as a good story. The best illustration of how this works is the daily market report produced by almost every general news publication, on or offline. Writing this summary of the day's trading is typically one of the first jobs a junior financial writer will be landed with – I know I was. It's a good education, because it involves reporting on any significant company reports or economic data releases, and any other news that might move the market. It can also be very challenging, because you might be left trying to churn out 400 words on why essentially nothing happened on a quiet day in August.

On a busy day, a good market report can provide a useful guide to how investors reacted to various bits of data and the overall 'theme' of that day's trading. On a quiet day, it can be as meaningless as a ritualistic reading of a sheep's entrails. Indeed, the market report is one of the best public examples of the folly of our pattern-spotting instincts and our love of stories. Take the typical commentary on daily oil price moves. If I had a penny for every time I've seen 'instability in the Middle East' used to explain oil price fluctuations (in either direction), then I'd have a nice big sweetie jar full of change. It makes intuitive sense – we all know that the Middle East produces lots of oil and that it's also unstable – so it's an easy one to nail things on. But, of course, it's nonsense – no one knows exactly why oil moves by a couple of cents a barrel on any given day.

Now, market reports are harmless enough. The narratives created within them are short-lived, throwaway little affairs. Most of us use them as one of many sources, rather than taking the information in them particularly seriously. But bigger stories, with more enduring narratives, are another matter. Typically, a group of stocks will start to outperform. Some people get rich. The story gets interesting. Readers want to know more about it. The promoters, experts and gurus in the sector start to get their names in the papers and their quotes in the stories. Stories about people getting rich by investing in the theme draw even more attention.

A positive feedback loop forms. Prices rise, journalists look for reasons for the rise, investors use the reasons as an excuse to buy more. What probably started out as a good story starts to get sensationalised and exaggerated in the telling. Initial scepticism peters out because prices just keep rising (this happened with the internet and, more recently, with cryptocurrencies). There's often a compelling supply-and-demand story that gets extrapolated out into eternity – and there's always a financial guru willing to make a big call to back that up with evidence from 'an expert' (during the commodity 'supercycle' of the 2000s, for example, Chinese demand for raw materials was apparently infinite). What was once novel and compelling becomes received wisdom.

This is all exacerbated by the fact that journalists often write at speed, on topics in which they themselves are not experts. So oversimplified, easily expressed arguments often win out over nuanced debate (the shorter the news cycle involved, and the more restricted the format, the worse it gets – this is why broadcast media tends to be more simplistic than print). This becomes even more of an issue when financial stories (which tend to be complicated at the best of times) become big enough to make the leap from the business pages to the front pages.

The good news is that this means that the generalist media is the closest thing to a reliable personification of the crowd that you'll find. By looking at the headlines you can work out very quickly what's foremost in people's minds. And if the economy is hitting the front pages, you have to start wondering about what kinds of misunderstandings are present, and which unforced errors are resulting from that. If editors and writers don't think that putting a direct comparison between London in the Blitz and a modern-day financial crash is an unreasonably hysterical thing to do, then what does that mean for market sentiment? Chances are, your average punter is in the process of liquidating their ISA and pension holdings in a fit of panic, and that as a result there's only so many people left to sell.

Going back to the concept of the 'metagame' (see chapter 3) again – reading the headlines is not about looking at the pieces on the board or analysing the fundamentals of the market. It's about getting an understanding of what the other players' mental models look like right now, thinking about how that will affect the course of play, and how you can take advantage of that.

To sum up: newspapers do not dictate the views of their readers. They reflect them. People want to read news that confirms their own world view and that addresses their concerns. This is key to understanding why the press can be such a powerful tool for sceptical investors. If the grim state of the economy is hitting the front page, then it's because a lot of people are worried about it.

And if a lot of people are worried about it, that means a lot of people know about it. And if a lot of people know about it, it's already in the price. And that means the only way to make money from the idea, is to bet against it.

Another way to look at it is like this: the media tends to focus on the outliers – that's what 'news' is, events that are out of the ordinary. The thing about outliers is that they tend to regress to the mean. Appearing on a magazine cover makes you an outlier – and it suggests that regression is not far behind.

So what specific features should you pay particular attention to? As I've said already, this is as much art as science, but here are some pointers on what to be aware of.

IT'S THE TONE, NOT THE CONTENT

A common mistake when considering the cover indicator is to read too much into the story that goes with it. You'll typically find with media stories that the headline is the most sensational aspect of the piece – it has to draw you in after all – and that the story itself is much more nuanced than the cover or headline might suggest. For example, if you read that *Economist* 'drowning in oil' cover story, it certainly doesn't say that cheap oil is going to last forever, and in fact it signs off by indicating any number of reasons why oil could easily go higher. Equally, when those who are 'long' an asset or company are confronted with the cover story indicator (gold in 2011 was a great example of this, when the once-hated asset graced several front pages and mainstream websites, before peaking in September that year), they'll often point to the content and argue that it doesn't reflect the bullish (or bearish) tone of the cover. But that doesn't matter. This is an impressionistic thing – if an obscure-ish asset like gold is on the front cover of a wide-circulation publication, it means too many people are interested in it. If an outlandish call, like 'Dow 36,000' can grace the cover of a serious magazine (the *Atlantic*, September 1999), then it shows that crowd sentiment has moved beyond the bounds of normality and rationality, and you should be on your guard.

The *Times* headline that morning in 2009 grabbed me, not because of the content – it was ultimately just yet another recession story – but because of the presentation. That was a point at which I could definitively say: "I know that it's not this bad, and that it's not going to get this bad."

BUY A PHYSICAL COPY

You should get your news via a physical newspaper where possible. One problem with the internet is that the news you see, and the wider online environment in which you operate, is tailor-made for you and your myriad cognitive biases. And that's not what you want – you want the news that everyone else is getting. The other advantage is that a newspaper makes the hierarchy of the stories very clear. The nearer the front of a section, the better-known – and the more 'priced-in' – the story already is. The flip side of finding contrarian ideas on the front pages is that you can also often find more interesting investment ideas bubbling under in the back pages. All in all, it's not a bad idea to read your paper from back to front (and I'm not talking about looking at the sports section before you read anything else).

SPECIALISTS VERSUS
NON-SPECIALISTS

A related point is to look out for stories that aren't where they should be. Business stories that have made it onto the front pages are a good example, or stories about how to set up your own tech business in the personal finance pages (as we saw during the dotcom boom). What this usually means is that a topic that's on the beat of a specialist journalist has gained enough coverage to catch the eye of a non-specialist. That's often a sign that a sector is destined for trouble. Why? The old stock market legend has it that Joseph Kennedy (John F. Kennedy's father, and a professional speculator) sold all of his shares just before the 1929 crash, after his shoeshine boy started giving him stock tips. Kennedy reasoned that if the shoeshine boys were giving share tips, the bull market had to be in its final throes. The logic is similar here – when journalists who don't normally cover investment or business are getting excited about a financial story, it means it has almost certainly reached a level of exposure where the price reflects unrealistic expectations (either positive or negative).

This is a point worth remembering about the flow of information in markets. It's true that most market-relevant information is available pretty much instantaneously these days for most participants. But not everyone pays attention to it right away. You can see this delayed reaction in individual stock prices, and you can certainly see it in the way that a mania creeps up on markets – where a genuinely good idea goes from being a buzzy, under-appreciated pocket of opportunity to a bloated, overhyped disaster waiting to happen.

IT'S NOT ABOUT QUALITY –
IT'S ABOUT QUANTITY

Following on from that point, bear in mind that the quality of a publication is not the issue here. It's the size of the audience. The bigger the readership, the more likely it is that the information contained is 'in the price'. This is the main reason that the *Economist* (and other wide-circulation current affairs magazines, but the *Economist* is probably the best example) is easily picked on as a contrarian cover indicator. It's in the sweet spot – it's a current affairs magazine that happens to have a lot of in-depth analysis on business and investment, rather than the other way around. And it has such a large global circulation that it can't help but represent the mainstream perspective – like a £1bn fund manager, it will struggle to go against the market, because in many ways it *is* the market. So if a story makes it on to the cover of the *Economist*, then by definition that means it's been widely disseminated. In effect, there can be no more 'unaware' buyers. Another point to remember is that mainstream newspapers are not in the business of selling genuinely contrarian ideas. When someone chooses to read a newspaper or political magazine regularly, they generally want to see their own biases reflected back at them. They don't want to be overly challenged. So if you want to get exposure to information that is less widely known, then it's worth looking at more obscure, specialist sources – these could include trade magazines and websites, research reports, or specialist information that you have access to as a result of your job, for example.

CHECK THE ORIGINAL SOURCES
FOR DISCREPANCIES

Being a journalist, I'm well aware of how the sausage is put together and I suspect that if many readers fully understood the process, they'd be surprised by how chaotic it can be. I used to work for a newswire. I would read all the economic news of the day and the company results as they were released, and turn them into stories which reporters on daily newspapers would often then read and use as the basis for their own stories. In the process of doing this, I would also refer to what my fellow newswire writers had written on the same subjects. I was often surprised by how different their interpretations were of the same raw material. What I deemed worth highlighting was not always even mentioned in another newswire piece. And sometimes I would find that they had come to virtually the opposite conclusion to me (bear in mind that these are not 'opinion' pieces – they are meant to be as objective as you get in the news business). So it's always worth checking the original sources, because at the very least you might find information that isn't elsewhere – and in some cases, you'll simply find that the reported version has missed the story entirely.

The good news is that almost every piece of financial news of consequence is derived from a source that is publicly available. That means that you can go back and check the information yourself, firsthand. Most releases of government data are not hard to understand with a little bit of research. As for corporate data, if you want to invest in individual companies then you need to be able to get to grips with reading and analysing a financial statement before you even think about doing so. That might sound like hard work, and that's because it is. But that's what you have to do if you want to spot things that the market hasn't spotted. You have to do the research. And the good thing about hard work is that most people don't like doing it, so they take shortcuts – including the professionals. Contrarian opportunities often arise because too many people assume that they are operating on the correct information, or because they want to believe in the prevailing wisdom because it suits them. They are often too lazy or busy to figure out whether or not they actually have the correct information. This is why it's always worth questioning the popular wisdom. Your job as a sceptical investor is to avoid making the same cognitive errors that everyone else does. So it's fine to get an idea from a magazine or even a newspaper, but you have to make it your own before you act on it. The media might be one of your first ports of call, but it should never be your last.

CHAPTER

8

The Incredible Power of Incentives

The 2008 financial crisis was caused by completely rational behaviour

IN 2008, THE global financial system came perilously close to collapse. There were many contributing factors, but ultimately, it came about as the direct result of mortgages in the US being handed out to people who couldn't possibly afford to pay them back. In one memorable example, a strawberry picker in California, earning just $15,000 a year, was loaned $720,000 to buy a 'McMansion' (as the new-builds springing up all over the US were nicknamed).

How on earth did it happen? It boils down to one thing.

Incentives.

Start at the top. The Federal Reserve, under the chairmanship of Alan Greenspan, had made it very clear by its actions during previous crashes, that when hard times loomed for markets, the US central bank would be ready to step in and cut interest rates. The 'Greenspan put' and the moral hazard it engendered incentivised investors to take greater risks than they otherwise would have, confident that the Fed had their backs.

Rising asset prices and falling interest rates made the quest for 'yield' an increasingly desperate affair. Investors who wanted to earn a higher interest rate on their investments without taking too much risk were finding it hard to do so. So when they were offered mortgage-backed securities that offered a higher yield than a 'risk-free' US Treasury, but enjoyed the same credit rating as US government debt, they jumped at the chance.

These securities consisted of bundles of mortgages. Credit rating agencies used flawed statistical models to prove that they could layer low-risk and high-risk mortgages together, then slice the resulting cake in such a way that holders of the slices earned a higher-than-average yield while taking lower-than-average risk. The top-tier credit rating given to these slices of debt meant that institutions could justify telling their yield-starved clients that they had found a way to get high returns for low risk.

The credit rating agencies however, were paid to rate these bonds by the banks who had created the mortgage-backed bonds in the first place. Clearly, there was an incentive there for the agencies to give the 'right' rating to these bundles in order to win more future business. The banks, meanwhile, facing steady demand from institutional investors, needed all the mortgages they could find in order to bundle them up to sell on. So they in turn were paying mortgage brokers to generate more business. Quantity was what mattered, so the brokers writing the loans had no regard for quality. The broker didn't care if the homeowner repaid the debt or not, because he was selling the mortgage to the banker. The banker didn't care, because she sold it to the institutional manager. The institutional manager didn't care, because the bank had paid the credit rating agency to rubber stamp the whole thing, so he had no reason to question the decision and took no responsibility for it.

In short, everyone involved got paid upfront, while the buck of the risk was passed right on down the chain to some other mug.

So 2008 made perfect sense, once you realise that all involved were merely responding to the incentives in front of them. Indeed, even the individuals who did the most to uncover the whole debacle – the hedge funds who bet against it – only did so because they had a huge incentive too: if they could figure out how to bet on the US housing market coming unstuck, they knew they could make a fortune (and many did).

How incentives can skew behaviour, for better or for worse

It's all too easy to see contrarianism as a strange and nebulous art. Anything that claims to deal with sentiment, or "animal spirits" as Keynes put it, can feel insubstantial, based on 'feels' rather than hard facts. But this isn't the case. The market is not given to 'fits of the vapours'. Investors may not always appear to act rationally, but there's usually an internal logic to even an apparently unhinged market. And if you can work out what it is, then you have a better chance of understanding where the market has got something 'wrong' and how to position yourself to benefit. Apparently irrational markets often boil down to individuals acting on incentives that make sense for them personally, even if they are catastrophic for the overall market or economy. As such, understanding incentives is one of the most potent tools in the armoury of the sceptical investor.

In his 1995 speech, 'The Psychology of Human Misjudgment', Charlie Munger (Warren Buffett's business partner) noted that: "I think I've been in the top 5% of my age cohort almost all my adult life in understanding the power of incentives, and yet I've always underestimated that power. Never a year passes but I get some surprise that pushes a little further my appreciation of incentive superpower." By way of example, Munger highlights how logistics giant Federal Express solved a problem with its night shift staff by changing their incentives. Fedex needed the staff in one airport to shift parcels between aeroplanes as rapidly and efficiently as possible, or else it would hold up the entire delivery process. The company struggled to make the system work until some bright spark realised that rather than paying the night staff per hour, they should pay them per shift, then let them go home as soon as the planes were all loaded. Given the incentive to get the job done fast, that's just what the workers did.

Of course, incentives can drive the wrong behaviour too. Take the recent example of Wells Fargo, a US bank in which (coincidentally) Buffett holds a large stake. Staff at the bank were paid bonuses according to the number of new products customers took out. As a result, many staff opened accounts in customers' names without their knowledge. The ensuing scandal hasn't destroyed the company, but it certainly hasn't been good for investors, nor for the bank's brand, which had benefited from being viewed as one of the 'least bad' banks in the wake of the financial crisis. As Matt Levine of Bloomberg points out, the company also probably lost a lot of good staff who either failed to open new accounts and so were fired, or struggled with the high-pressure sales culture.

These examples highlight both the power of incentives and how tricky it is to design effective incentive schemes. It's also important to remember that incentives are not purely external or financial. We have internal motivating forces too. We have a desire to be perceived to be consistent in our behaviour, and to attain social approval (of which the desire for consistency is part). This desire in itself is by no means inherently noble and, as we discussed in chapter 5, can certainly lead to destructive behaviour (such as the herding instinct that sceptical investors try to resist). However, in normal circumstances you might expect this internal motivation to prevent someone from doing something immoral or socially unacceptable such as, say, opening a bank account in another person's name without their permission.

But this internal incentive to behave in a socially acceptable way can be entirely short-circuited by external incentives, and sometimes in unexpected ways. There's a well-known study from 2000 ('A Fine is a Price' by Uri Gneezy of University of California, and Aldo Rustichini of University of Minnesota, published in *The Journal of Legal Studies*) which looked at a nursery which had problems with parents coming in late to pick up their kids. The nursery started to fine the latecomers – and the problem became even worse. Whereas previously the parents would try to avoid the social disapproval and stigma of selfishness that went along with picking their kids up late, they now regarded the fine as a price to be paid for permission to be late. In effect, being late turned into a transaction rather than a transgression. So payment can effectively license behaviour that would otherwise be socially unacceptable (on a much more dramatic level, you can compare it to the blood payments made to wronged families in old feudal and tribal societies, whereby a social obligation – vengeance – is replaced by a financial one).

This ability of money (and other external incentives) to short-circuit intrinsic motivators, including both conscience and common sense, is known as the 'undermining effect'. Even if you don't believe you are motivated strongly by money, it does provide a pretty clear signpost as to what you are expected to do by your employer. Systems and incentives also give us the shortcuts we crave to avoid expending valuable resources on thinking or making moral judgements or taking responsibility. Indeed, the very existence of a system or a process creates a certain amount of moral hazard by allowing individuals to dispense with personal responsibility and just follow the rules. If you've ever wondered how people end up driving into rivers because their GPS tells them to do so – there's your answer.

So it's the very effectiveness of incentive schemes that makes it vital to design them well. That's hard to do, even for what Michael Mauboussin describes as jobs that are heavy on "algorithmic" tasks – ones that involve a relatively clear goal and an obvious list of steps to take to reach that goal. But it becomes even harder when you're looking at jobs with lots of complexity (what Mauboussin calls "heuristic" tasks). Indeed, it's one reason why the ongoing scandal of chief executive pay may be one of the most destructive elements of today's corporate culture.

CEO pay, misaligned incentives and the damage it does

Perhaps the biggest and most obvious incentive issue in investment is the agency problem. When applied to listed companies, this simply describes the fact that the people who run the company (the management team) are not the ones who own the company (the shareholders). In theory, an owner lives or dies according to the performance of the business, so they want it to run as efficiently as possible. A manager, on the other hand, at their most cynical, has every incentive to do the minimum amount of work necessary to claim their salary. They may also be less inclined to take tough decisions on managing resources efficiently – as Mike Dariano, who writes The Waiter's Pad blog, puts it: "Leaders who aren't owners prefer more to less."

The obvious solution – or so it seems – is to align the incentives by turning executives into owners. And over time, this is precisely what has happened. As Mauboussin pointed out more than a decade ago: "In the mid-1980s, virtually no chief executive pay was tied to the stock price. By the mid-1990s, that ratio – fueled by employee stock option grants – surpassed 40%." Now, roughly 70% of CEO pay is related to stock market performance. As a result of all this, CEO pay has rocketed relative to the pay packets taken home by the typical staff member. That exacerbates concerns about the wealth gap and the social fabric, which is arguably reason enough to avoid it. But even if you don't care about that, the other problem is that evidence shows that it simply doesn't work. You only have to look at shareholder returns over the same period to see that the rewards accruing to executives have risen far more rapidly than the share prices of their companies in general. Moreover, a July 2016 study of large listed US companies by index provider MSCI suggested that between 2006 and 2015, the more a company paid its CEO, the less well it did. Those with the lowest CEO pay relative to the industry average soundly thrashed those in the top quintile.

Why does this happen? Firstly, managing a company is a complicated job – it's "heuristic" intensive, to use the jargon.

There is no specific action (such as 'build more widgets') that can be targeted as a performance measure. Ideally, a CEO needs the flexibility to react to rapidly changing circumstances and to deal with unforeseen threats and opportunities in a creative, adaptive manner. Instead, by imposing an external incentive scheme, you immediately short-circuit the CEO's intrinsic motivation, common sense and sense of duty or pride in simply doing a good job, in favour of focusing tightly on maximising whatever it takes to get the money. In effect, you substitute an efficient, flexible internal reward scheme for an inefficient, inflexible external scheme.

Secondly, how do you measure CEO performance? Clearly the share price is one way, although it's not an ideal gauge – lots of things impact on a company's share price, from the economic big picture to general investor sentiment to monetary policy, and the CEO has very little if any control over any of those factors. So companies have also tended to settle on earnings per share (EPS) as an easy way to measure CEO performance. The idea is that, ultimately, the CEO's job is to increase shareholder value and the most obvious measure of that is the amount of profit the company is making. However, as Mauboussin wrote back in 2005 (and it really hasn't changed): "Rather than internalizing the principles of shareholder value, many managers ... defaulted to a near-messianic focus on EPS growth".

The problem is that there are plenty of ways to boost EPS, many of which are destructive in the long run. You can cut research and development spending, and any other investment spending that is necessary for the health of the business in the long run, but which cuts into profits in the short term. You can run out and buy a rival company with borrowed money to artificially boost your earnings per share – your core business might be struggling, but you can mask that by bolting on another business. Or you can fiddle the figures by using entirely legal accounting conventions to shift bad news into a future set of results and bring good news forward (more on that in a moment). Or you can use financial engineering – borrow money, buy back shares, reducing the share count and automatically boosting EPS.

Economist and author Andrew Smithers has even argued that the structure of executive pay is one of the key drivers of the problem of sluggish productivity in many developed countries – a desire to prop up EPS and share prices in the short term has resulted in chronic under-investment and stifled innovation, because innovation is expensive in the short term.

There are also some straightforward common-sense objections to the scale of executive pay packets. How motivated can any individual be when they have the potential to earn life-changing sums of money in just a few years at the top? The brutal truth is that once you've made a level of generational wealth – once you know that you could quit tomorrow and never have to work again – then you don't have to worry about what happens in five years' time. And regardless of how big your ego is, working to pay the mortgage is always going to be a bigger incentive than working because you want to have a bigger yacht than the CEO down the road. No one put it better than Jimmy Cayne, ex-CEO of Bear Stearns, which – other than Lehman Brothers – was probably the single most-disgraced bank of the financial crisis. He spoke to financial journalist William D. Cohan around the time of the crisis (who recalled the conversation in a 2015 article for *Vanity Fair*). Cayne lost a billion dollars in paper net worth when Stearns collapsed. But he was still worth more than $600m. As he put it, says Cohan: "The only people [who] are going to suffer are my heirs, not me ... Because when you have a billion six and you lose a billion, you're not exactly, like, crippled, right?" In short, a huge pay packet is arguably a distraction from doing a good job, not an incentive.

Why don't shareholders do anything about this? Mainly because many of them are 'agents' too. The ownership structure of the market has changed dramatically over the years – where once individuals accounted for the majority of shareholders in individual stocks, now institutions are the big owners. And the fund managers employed by these institutions are happy to focus on short-term boosts to the share price of their holdings, because most of them are measured on their short-term results too. Perhaps more to the point, most of them are paid highly as well, and see no reason to focus on egregious pay packets lest attention be paid to their own. In short, nobody directly involved in setting CEO pay has any particular incentive to restrict it.

There are signs – driven mainly by the mounting sense of frustration, following the 2008 banking bailout, that executives get away with taking their money and running when times get hard (an irritation which is understandable) – that this is changing. Under pressure from governments, who in turn are being squeezed by angry voters, fund managers (big passive managers in particular) are making more noises about corporate governance and shareholder pay. But don't hold your breath for radical change.

What can you do about this?

There are a number of things you can do to spot and avoid companies where the manager or employee incentives are going badly wrong or have the potential to do so.

- **What is this person being paid to do and do they have confidence in their ability to do it?** Firstly, check out the remuneration report on any company you plan to invest in. If you're baffled by it – if you can't work out how much the executive team is getting paid, or what they're getting paid for – then look elsewhere. One thing to remember about investing in individual companies is that there are always plenty of fish in the sea and a limited number that you can realistically keep tabs on at any given time. So you're always looking for excuses not to buy in – confusing remuneration is a valid one, as is unnecessary complexity in general. Also, a good rule of thumb is to look at 'skin in the game' – what proportion of the company's shares does the executive team, and the CEO in particular, own? If it's pretty insubstantial, or worse still, none at all, then why should you invest yourself given the CEO's wariness?

- **Watch out for empire building:** acquisitiveness is not always a bad sign – some very good companies have made superb returns by consolidating their sectors and making better use of resources than previous owners did. But on average, acquisitions are bad news. They are often a sign that the market in general is getting overheated – everyone is focusing on the potential upside rather than the risks, and so they are ripe to be seduced by the fee-hungry flatterers in investment banks.

Moreover, they often suggest that the CEO's ego is getting out of hand (witness the empire building in the banking sector that preceded the crash of 2008), and also that they have run out of better ideas for boosting earnings per share. It's a good sign of a weak board stuffed with nodding dogs who won't challenge the boss. A CEO can't be overly cautious – that's not their purpose – but as Buffett puts it: "A board's real job is to find the right CEO and prevent him or her from overreaching. Not much else matters." Telling the difference between a good and a bad acquisition is often simply a matter of timing. Is the target cheap or expensive? Is M&A activity in general low or high? If M&A is booming and the market is expensive, just play the odds – it's very likely to be a duff acquisition and you should act accordingly.

- **Watch out for surprisingly consistent outperformance:** an interesting academic paper came out in 2017 called 'A Reputation for Beating Analysts' Expectations and the Slippery Slope to Earnings Manipulation', from Jenny Chu and researchers at the universities of Cambridge, Southern California, Hong Kong and Houston. They looked at all US-listed companies between 1985 and 2010 that had been censured by the US regulator, the Securities and Exchange Commission (SEC), for manipulating their earnings. They found that in the lead-up to being pulled up by the regulator, the stocks had been more likely to beat analysts' quarterly earnings forecasts consistently, both during the manipulation period (as you'd expect) but also in the three years prior to it. In other words, if companies are going to start fiddling the figures, they typically do it after they've had a good long run of beating the market, and are under pressure from high market expectations. The academics also found that the more concentrated power is within these companies – i.e. the less accountable the CEO is to anyone else in the organisation – the more likely it is that the company will succumb to the temptation to manipulate its earnings in order to accrue more stock market acclaim.

This makes sense. Like everyone else, CEOs like to have a consistent world view of themselves. If the share price, their pay packets, and investment analysts keep saying that they're geniuses, they'll struggle not to believe the hype. So when things start to go wrong, they believe that a) they'll be able to fix it, and b) want to maintain that consistency. So it's very easy to fall into the temptation of fiddling the figures. One of the main things to keep an eye on here is changes to the accounting methods used by a successful company (particularly a fast-growing one). These include one-off (exceptional) items that don't seem to be one-offs, or changes to policies on the treatment of balance sheet assets, or a deterioration in cash flows, for example. But also be aware of the simple fact that nothing goes up or down in a straight line. If a company is enjoying a suspiciously smooth ascent, then – well, be suspicious.

Skin in the game and corporate structure: why is this company listed in the first place?

It's also worth looking at how a company has come to market and what this says about the likely incentive structures.

- **Family firms:** one reason that people like to invest in family firms is that the owners – the family – tend to be a lot more engaged. This is not to say that family firms are inherently good – the mixing of personal life and business life means that these companies can come undone for any number of unusual reasons stemming from domestic squabbles. They may also have a cavalier attitude towards minority shareholders (this is often one of the biggest problems with investing in emerging markets). However, the successful ones have a good incentive to think for the long term – there is a lot of pride tied up in a successful family business and once it has survived long enough to go public, no generation wants to be the one that wiped out the familial cash cow. So the family is likely to focus on the long-term health of the business, which means taking into account a wider range of stakeholders and factors beyond the short-term share price.

- **Be sceptical of IPOs:** if you fancy the look of an IPO (initial public offering – when a company sells its shares on the market for the first time), ask yourself one question: 'Why does the vendor want to sell now?' A founder goes public for lots of reasons, but you should start from the assumption that if it's a good time for a well-informed owner to be a seller of an asset, then it is probably a bad time to be the buyer of that asset. There's a reason why rising IPOs are a sign of a bullish market – it's because investors are more receptive to paying over the odds for unproven companies. There are of course exceptions, but do you have the time or skill to hunt them down? As Buffett (again) puts it: "An IPO is like a negotiated transaction – the seller chooses when to come public – and it's unlikely to be a time that's favourable to you. So, by scanning 100 IPOs, you're way less likely to find anything interesting than scanning an average group of 100 stocks."

- **Private equity cast-offs:** approach private equity sales with ten times the scepticism you'd apply to any other IPO. Not all private equity deals are bad, but in many cases, companies are effectively hollowed out by the substitution of equity for debt, then chucked back to the undiscriminating hordes in the public markets when the investment cycle is reaching a peak. Another rule of thumb is that you're better investing alongside private equity (via an investment trust, say) rather than buying from private equity. And in both cases, you want to avoid getting involved near the top of the cycle – do it when no one else wants to touch it.

- **The demise of the listed sector, and overly controlling founders:** in light of all this, it's interesting to note that one feature of shareholder capitalism in the US over the last few years has been companies – especially in the tech sector – refusing to come to market before they are relatively mature, because they want to focus on building the business and taking long-term decisions, and they don't feel that public markets are the best place to do that. This may be best epitomised by

Amazon. When Amazon came to market, CEO Jeff Bezos effectively told his shareholders that Amazon would forever be expanding into new markets, so they had better be prepared to never get to the point where the company gave a damn about maximising shareholder returns. 'Trust me' was the mantra. It's worked so far, and it's certainly hard to accuse Amazon of making decisions based on short-term quarterly earnings. But while Bezos relies on getting his own way by being upfront with shareholders and demonstrating that his approach works, other tech founders have tried to raise funds for expansion while maintaining an iron grip on their companies by issuing different classes of shares. Their own shares have perhaps ten times the voting rights of the ordinary shares, and some share classes may have no voting rights at all. Both Facebook and Google's founders own shares which give them effective control even while owning a minority of the company, while Snap, the founder of messaging service Snapchat, went public with shares that offered investors no voting rights at all. The cryptocurrency-related ICO (initial coin offering) movement (whereby what I hesitate to describe as 'investors' give companies money in exchange for tokens that give them the right to purchase goods or services rather than any stake in the company itself) is almost a logical extension of this shift. Thankfully the companies that manage the major stock market indices are trying to make a stand against these sorts of structures (Snap was excluded from the S&P 500 for example), but it's worth monitoring.

How Sir John Templeton made over $100m by understanding incentives

Before we leave this topic, let's look at another one of Sir John Templeton's contrarian triumphs, carried out much later in his investing career than the second-world-war experience we looked at in chapter 1. Here's the trade: in the first half of 2000, at the very height of the dotcom bubble, Templeton knew that the market was extraordinarily overpriced. As he told *Forbes* magazine in May 2001: "This is the only time in my 88 years when I saw technology stocks go to 100 times earnings; or, when there were no earnings, 20 times sales. It was insane, and I took advantage of the temporary insanity. I never thought I'd see a mania like that happen again in my life."[1]

You might be thinking: 'So what? Anyone could see that tech stocks were overvalued at that point.' The difference is that Templeton figured out how to profit from that fact. He picked out 84 stocks, and invested an average of $2.2m in each, betting that their prices would fall. Within a year, he had made more than $100m on the trade. More than half of the stocks that he bet on fell in price by 95% or more. It was a stunningly profitable trade.

It was also extraordinarily risky. Shorting stocks is much more dangerous than betting on them rising. As long as you don't use leverage, you can buy and hold a stock for as long as you want without incurring anything beyond opportunity cost (which is an important cost, but not one that will actively force you to sell a stock when you don't want to). You can't do that when you're short. So if you plan to make money by going short, then you have to get your timing right. Betting against a bubble market – regardless of how overvalued you think it might be – is particularly dangerous. Tech stocks had been overpriced for a long time.

So how did Templeton manage to both call the market correctly and profit from it? He looked for stocks that were selling for three times the price that they first went public at – in other words, they were egregiously overvalued, even by the standards of tech stocks at the time. He then established short positions in those stocks. But here's the key. He had looked at the incentive packages of the founders of these companies. And the positions that Templeton had taken in their stocks were designed to kick in 11 days before 'lockup expirations'. That's the point at which the insiders – the people who had stock when the company first went public – were first allowed to sell their shares and cash in. Templeton correctly assumed that it would take a very, very confident, patient or delusional founder to hang on to shares that were priced at three times their original expectations, and which most professionals thought were overvalued in the first place.

So in this case, the valuation was the easy part. The clever part, the part that gave Templeton his edge, was in understanding the prevailing incentive structure of the day, and realising that it gave him a very clear guide as to what would likely trigger the collapse in these stocks, and how and when it would happen. And that takes us to the final, golden rule of understanding incentives – **find the path of least resistance**. If you want to know what individuals – from central bankers to executives – will do in a given situation, then find the path of least resistance, the choice that they find least painful. Now clearly, this varies from person to person. Someone who does not take what the average person would perceive as the path of least resistance is usually considered to have character (or is just plain ornery, as Americans might put it). But on average – and averages are what we're dealing with in the stock market – the path of least resistance is the one that involves the least pain. It explains why central bankers prefer to cut rates rather than raise them, why politicians would rather tax you by stealth than in a transparent manner, and why CEOs get paid so much more than they're worth.

CHAPTER

9

The Importance of Intellectual Humility

H UGH HENDRY IS probably the closest that the hedge fund industry has ever come to producing a working-class hero. The son of a Glasgow lorry driver and a receptionist mother, he's forthright in a manner not often seen in the City (or on *Newsnight*), unafraid of controversy, and happy to use his aggressive and eloquent arguing style to run rings around his opponents. His personal style reflects his investment style – punchy, backed by well-considered arguments, and deeply contrarian. Hendry not only saw the credit crisis coming, but also positioned his portfolio for what he saw as the inevitable outcome – a deflationary depression in which bond yields would collapse, share prices would tumble and banks would go bust. As a result, his hedge fund returned more than 30% in 2008, at a time when the S&P 500 fell by 40% and most people's diversified portfolios turned out only to be diversified in theory, rather than practice.

It was an incredible performance and it made his reputation at a time when most people outside the financial system had been completely blindsided. It also helped that Hendry presented his investment views within a framework that pitched him (and hedge funds in general) as crusaders against the laziness, moral turpitude and vested interests endemic to the financial and economic establishment. It was a compelling narrative – the hedge fund manager as Robin Hood – topped off by Hendry claiming on *Newsnight* that Nobel Prize winner Joseph Stiglitz "didn't know what he was talking about" and calling former Danish prime minister Poul Rasmussen a "champagne socialist".

Unfortunately, Hendry's extraordinary performance did not continue. He remained bearish long after central banks had started to print money, which did him no favours during the epic rally that began in March 2009. His warnings that the worst was yet to come made sense to many amid the wreckage of the financial crisis, and concerns that central banks had merely patched over the worst of the immediate damage were entirely valid. The fact that the culprits had got away scot-free also meant that his anger touched a chord. However, it could no longer be described as a contrarian view. And while it seemed logical to expect a further crisis – a view given further credence by the eurozone's near-meltdown over Greece – the market just kept going up.

I had a lot of sympathy with Hendry's views myself. The 2008 crash had felt like the inevitable outcome of a hubristic system overreaching itself. And there was an undeniable moral dimension to it all. Driven by loose monetary policies, society had neglected the values of hard work and thrift, and instead borrowed prosperity from the future to squander on driving up the prices of unproductive assets – property in particular. And having been proved right about the pending credit crunch, people like me got cocky. 2008 was just the start. The collapse wouldn't stop, because the rot went too deep. If society didn't pay the bill that was due, a worse downturn was just around the corner.

But as it turned out, it wasn't. And anyone who clung to the belief that it was, missed out on making a huge amount of money. Between 2009 and 2014, simply investing in a cheap S&P 500 tracker fund would have comfortably more than doubled your money. Over that same period, Hendry's hedge fund made no money at all, despite a good showing in 2011, when the eurozone crisis was at its height.

So what went wrong? In 2014, Merryn Somerset Webb (my colleague at *MoneyWeek*) interviewed Hendry for a series of online videos that represented something of a relaunch for the hedge fund manager. The first in the series was one of the most excoriating self-assessments I've ever seen from a fund manager. Hendry admitted: "I found myself unable to forgive the Federal Reserve and the other central banks for ... bailing out Wall Street from the excess of 2008. I just couldn't get over it." He talks about "luxuriating in the polemics" of various well-known bearish commentators, such as Marc Faber (a serial predictor of epic crashes, and writer of the *Gloom, Boom and Doom* newsletter). "I luxuriated as they ranted and it was fine for them to rant. But I am charged with the responsibility of making money and not being some moral guardian and certainly not a moral curmudgeon."

Hendry's Damascene conversion – the point in 2013 when he learned to stop worrying and love central bankers, as it were – helped to turn around his performance somewhat. However, overall, he struggled to adjust – he lost 4% in 2016, and after shedding nearly 10% in the first eight months of 2017, he eventually shut down his fund, admitting that "it wasn't supposed to be like this". By the time it was closed down, assets under management (the amount of money he was managing for investors) had dwindled from a high of well over $1bn in 2013, to just above $30m.

Two major things went wrong here. One is only really relevant to existing or aspiring fund managers – from a professional view,

Hendry should have stuck with being a bear market fund. Most asset allocators will forgive mediocre returns during a bull market if they think the fund will enjoy double-digit returns during a bear market – that helps them to tick the diversification box. By effectively turning bullish, Hendry rattled those investors – they could no longer be sure of his precise strategy, or that he would outperform come the inevitable hard times.

But the other issue is applicable to any investor, because it's one of the fundamental challenges that goes with being a successful sceptic. If you are willing to go against the crowd consistently, then you are already primed to believe that you know better than the rest. You have to be, or else you wouldn't go against them. And as we considered in chapter 5, you have to be hard-headed and at least a little stubborn to hold your nerve in the face of all that opprobrium. If you then make out like a bandit while everyone else is whimpering every time they open their portfolio statements, then this stubbornness and sense of superior understanding will only be reinforced by the fact you've been proved right. The danger then is that you fall into the trap of thinking: 'I'm right, and everyone else is an idiot.' You become convinced that your own world view – the one that made you all that money – is still correct. You fail to engage with the changing circumstances around you. You fail to recognise that your once-contrarian outlook is no longer a bold, minority take, but in fact the dominant paradigm.

As Hendry learned to his cost, you get so used to fighting your corner that it's incredibly easy – without really even being entirely aware of it – to imagine that you are still arguing from the perspective of the underdog, rather than the consensus. You end up wallowing in confirmation bias, and savouring your victory, rather than wondering about what happens next. Yet all the while the world keeps moving beneath your feet. This sort of hubris and intellectual arrogance is arguably the most insidious threat to the successful contrarian. So how can you spot it coming – and how can you avoid falling prey to it?

Hubris, meet Nemesis: five warning signs for sceptical investors

1. YOU DISMISS ARGUMENTS THAT YOU DON'T WANT TO HEAR

Hendry points out that he "luxuriated" in well-written polemics issued by writers he agreed with. As US financial writer Morgan Housel puts it: "The cosiest spot is under the warm blanket of ideology." If you find yourself feeling relieved when a new piece of work from one of your favourite writers comes out, and you're constantly putting it to the top of your pile, and avoiding research that doesn't concur with your views, then there's a problem. Remember – what makes you feel comfortable rarely makes you money.

2. YOU ARE NEVER, EVER BULLISH

Bull markets are more common than bear markets (certainly within the lifetimes of most of the people who I imagine are reading this book). So contrarian views often have a bearish tinge, simply because the market tends to go up over time. Bearish views also appeal to those who like to identify as rugged individualists. They almost always sound more sophisticated, more worldly wise, and better informed than anyone else. It's surprisingly easy to sound like a hardbitten realist when you're talking about the end of the world and sneering at the 'sheeple' who can't see it coming (by the way, use of the word 'sheeple' is another surefire indicator that whatever your view is, it's wrong). It's much harder to pull off the hardbitten last cowboy act, when all you're doing is arguing tentatively that a grim-looking situation is about to get a little bit better, and so it's probably a good time to buy.

As a result, it's easy for sceptics – particularly the more moralistically inclined – to slip unthinkingly over the line into being 'permabears'. If you find yourself falling into this trap, just remember – it's easier to destroy than to create. It's easier to carp from the sidelines than to do. It's easier to be the cynical edgy pessimist than the one who's willing to take the risk of being labelled a cockeyed optimist for daring to look on the bright side. Scepticism is healthy and will often lead you to be rightly bearish on certain markets or sectors. But cynicism is just a psychological defence mechanism against disappointment. Don't mistake one for the other. As John Stuart Mill put it: "I know that it is thought essential to a man who has any knowledge of the world to have an extremely bad opinion of it … I have observed that not the man who hopes when others despair, but the man who despairs when others hope, is admired by a large class of persons as a sage, and wisdom is supposed to consist not in seeing further than other people, but in not seeing so far."

3. YOU DON'T MIND BEING WRONG BECAUSE YOU 'DISAPPROVE' OF THE MARKET

An extension of the romanticisation of the bearish view is that a certain type of contrarian likes to see themselves as a heroic figure, wielding their sword of truth against the battalions of vested interests in their quest for economic and financial sanity. And many bets against the market do start out from that desire. A contrarian sees something wrong – a neurotic national obsession with property, a deeply flawed financial system, a borderline fraudulent business model – and they make it their mission to argue against that 'wrong' in the market. This can be a good thing. Many fraudulent companies have been hastened to a sticky and deserved end by hard-working short sellers.

But the market is not a morality play. If a position is costing you money, and you're tempted to shrug it off because you're outraged at the way the market works, then you need to get over yourself. If you're angry, write a letter to your MP. If you want to make money by arguing about your principles with people who won't listen, then go into politics or the priesthood. If you want to make money in markets, then pay attention to the facts on the ground rather than your own prejudices.

Do not make moral judgements about markets. (This does not preclude ethical investing by the way – if you want to avoid tobacco stocks or whatever, that's a different topic.) I've seen many good investors and smart thinkers paralysed by their rage against 'the system' and by investing on the basis of how the world should be rather than how it is. Quantitative easing may be immoral and the source of a great deal of wealth inequality.

Government subsidies can and do distort the market in favour of certain sectors. You don't have to like it, and you can complain about it or even campaign against it – but if you want to make money, you have to take those facts into account whether you approve or not, and invest accordingly.

4. YOU ARE THROWING BLAME AT EVERYONE ELSE

In the process of writing this book, I read an interview with one of the few truly great fund managers out there. This man has a fantastic track record, but he had also held onto one particular stock – a serial disappointer – for far too long. The journalist asked him about it. In a somewhat grumpy manner, he acknowledged that he wasn't terribly pleased with the stock, but he also claimed to be annoyed that other investors and "the media" (one of the best catch-all villains, I'm sure you'll agree) were rooting for this company to fail.

Any time that someone blames the media or short sellers for the failings of a company or sector, your bullshit indicator should be going haywire – particularly if that person is you. If you feel defensive about something, then you're trying to avoid something. The truth is that if the papers have something wrong, then reality will out. Indeed, you should welcome the occasions when the media misunderstands a stock, because it gives you the opportunity to buy in cheap. So if you are feeling rattled about a holding, and keen to lash out when challenged on it, you should audit your emotions and work out why that is. Is it because you are worried that you have made a mistake? And if so, then why? Revisit the holding. Go back to your investment journal. Are the reasons you bought the stock still valid? Would you buy it again today? If not, maybe it's time to stop blaming other factors and accept that you called it wrong.

5 . NO ONE DISAGREES WITH YOU ANYMORE

If the market has done what you said it would do, then your view is not contrarian anymore. It's nice to be right. It's nice to be popular and to enjoy your time in the sunshine, particularly after ploughing a lonely intellectual furrow. It's nice to be able to shake your fist and say 'I told you so!' But if everyone is clamouring to hear your opinion, and agreeing with it, that means they don't disagree with you anymore. If your view is now the new mainstream, you need to consider why that is. Circumstances have clearly changed. Does that invalidate your current view? That stock that everyone laughed at you for owning – they're not laughing anymore. Does that suggest that you should buy more? Or – as is far more likely – does it suggest that it's time to look for the best opportunity to take your hard-won profits and look for a new trade?

How the world's smartest man learned to be a humble investor

Most of these problems are rooted in confirmation bias – the difficulty in letting go of hard-won views, particularly ones that have proven successful in the face of adversity. And everyone suffers from it – from the least ideological amateur investor to opinionated old pros. So how can you resist it – or at least prevent it from handicapping your investment performance?

The answer is to cultivate intellectual humility – to recognise the possibility that you are wrong, and take steps to change your approach, rather than defending your view to the death.

I'll explain how to do that in a moment, but I don't want you to start thinking that intellectual humility means donning a hair shirt and beating yourself up after every failed trade. So first I want to give you an example of someone who did successfully change his investment approach after a humbling experience at the hands of the market – John Maynard Keynes.

Keynes is best known, of course, for being one of the most important figures in economics. But as we noted back in chapter 1, he was also a prolific, and eventually, very successful investor. When Keynes (allegedly – there is in fact no primary source that I'm aware of for this quote) warned that "the market can remain irrational longer than you can remain solvent", he was speaking from experience.

Keynes was perhaps the last human being on earth that you would naturally describe as possessing intellectual humility. Both his education and his temperament led him to feel that he was a man apart from the norm – a cut above, both intellectually and morally. The son of a pair of upper-middle-class academics, he won a scholarship to Eton and excelled. As Robert L. Heilbroner observes in a review of Robert Skidelsky's biography of Keynes in the *New York Times*, "Keynes won nearly every competition he ever entered, a performance not likely to encourage humility in a developing personality." He was also deeply contrarian. He had no respect for conventional sexual or social attitudes (notes Heilbroner: "The aristocracy he regarded as absurd ... the proletariat as 'boorish'."), but nor was he a 'conventional' bohemian – he was regarded as something of an outsider and as too close to the establishment by fellow members of the artsy Bloomsbury group. Then there's the fact that, like many of his peers, he was a keen eugenicist up until he died – you don't get much more intellectually arrogant than believing that you have the right (the responsibility, even) to promote selective breeding among the lower orders.

In short, Keynes believed he was smarter than the crowd, and as such, he thought he could outsmart them. And in his early investment career, that's what he aimed to do. He was a speculator. In *A Treatise on Money* (1930), Keynes noted that (my emphasis added) "it may often profit the wisest to anticipate mob psychology rather than the real trend of events, and **to ape unreason** ... so long as the crowd can be relied on to act in a certain way, even if it be misguided, it will be to the advantage of the better-informed professional to act in the same way – a short period ahead." And in a letter to his fellow Bloomsbury-ite Lytton Strachey in 1905, he airily suggested of the market, that "it is so easy ... to master the principles of these things."

Keynes grasped that crowds were psychologically flawed (the idea of market efficiency was a while away into the future) and there was nothing wrong with that view. The trouble was, he took the wrong lesson from it. He was arrogant enough to believe that he could not only anticipate the errors of the crowd, but that he could also then copy those errors before the crowd had even made them, thus profiting from their predictable mistakes. In short, he decided the path to profits was to second-guess the market – rather than to focus on the gap between expectations and fundamentals – and he believed that it would be a simple enough task to remain one step ahead of the fools he was competing with.

For a while, he did fine with this approach. He had the insouciant approach to money that only those who've never lacked or lost it can enjoy. In 1920, he wrote to his mother: "Money is a funny thing … [with] a little extra knowledge and experience of a special kind, it simply keeps rolling in." In another letter to his father, he wrote: "Win or lose, this high stakes gambling amuses me." It's the sort of casual-yet-secretly-thrilled boast that you hear from anyone who happens to get lucky when they start out trading or investing – 'This is easy, I don't know why anyone says it isn't.' It's also usually a sure sign that they're going to come a cropper further down the line.

Keynes was already involved in helping with the investments of various institutions, including King's College, Cambridge, his alma mater. Fortunately for them, while he used the same sort of investing style as for his own portfolio, he didn't bet as aggressively. He suffered losses on his own portfolio in 1920, and then in 1928, he was wiped out in a commodities crash, which forced him to sell the majority of his share portfolio. The remnants of said portfolio were then almost entirely lost in the crash of 1929. As Justyn Walsh notes in his book, *Keynes and the Market*, Keynes' net worth fell by more than 80% to less than £8,000.

Keynes was lucky enough to have the resources to draw upon to start again. But he was also intellectually humble enough to shift strategy, rather than trying to pursue the same doomed system. He noted that his market-timing system (which he'd given the somewhat grandiose name of "credit cycling") required "abnormal foresight" and "phenomenal skill". He would later go on to explain, in a memo to King's College estates committee, that attempting to time the market "is for various reasons impracticable and indeed undesirable. Many of those who attempt it sell too late and buy too late, and do both too often, incurring heavy expenses and developing too unsettled and speculative a state of mind". As you can see, this is hardly a humble shift of mind. Keynes doesn't say: 'I can't do this.' Instead, he disowns his previous strategy as being impractical for anyone. It's this ability to change his mind without overly agonising about it, or taking it as a personal insult to his clearly colossal ego, that sets Keynes apart.

He realised that investment success for him hinged not on second-guessing the crowd but on his spotting inexpensive yet promising companies that had been neglected by the market, investing in them, and being patient (value investing, in other words – which we'll look at in chapter 13). In the same memo to King's, he outlined his new approach. He now preferred to hold "a careful selection of a few investments ... having regard to their cheapness in relation to their probably actual and potential intrinsic value over a period of years ahead and in relation to alternative investments at the time." And in 1944, he emphasised the need to avoid what was popular, in a letter to Sir Jasper Ridley (at Eton). "The central principle of investment is to go contrary to the general opinion, on the grounds that if everyone agreed about its merit, the investment is inevitably too dear and therefore unattractive." In other words, he found situations where it was clear to him that the crowd was wrong, and then he settled back to wait until the crowd woke up to its error. Within six years, he had recovered spectacularly from his earlier losses, notes Walsh, "parlaying net assets of just under £8,000 at the end of 1929 to more than £500,000 only six years later."

Overall, according to performance data compiled by the London Business School's David Chambers and Elroy Dimson, Keynes managed annualised returns of around 5.7% between 1924 and 1932. But after changing his style, from 1933 until his death in 1946, he made closer to 13% a year. That's an impressive return, made all the more impressive by the fact that it was achieved during a time period that included the second world war, and also that it was achieved without dividend reinvestment – the dividends were used to provide an income for the college. When he took over as bursar of King's College, Cambridge in 1924, the college had £285,000 in funds. By the time he died in 1946, the pot had grown to £1.2m.

Now, I'm not saying that you'll make that sort of money – but if one of the most snobbish men in recent history can cultivate sufficient intellectual humility and flexibility to shift from a losing investment strategy to a hugely successful one, then you can too.

How to be more humble

Intellectual humility is a recognised psychological trait. It refers to our capacity to question the veracity of our own beliefs and to adjust them when we're presented with new information. In other words, it's our best defence against confirmation bias.

As Michael Mauboussin puts it, "good thinking requires maintaining as accurate a view of the world as possible". And that means adopting an intellectually humble mindset. According to one of the leading researchers in the field, Mark Leary of Duke University, those with high levels of intellectual humility are open to new ideas, generally curious, tolerant of ambiguity, and recognise that both their own and other's beliefs are fallible – they don't think less of other people who change their minds on a subject, or who have a different view to their own. Dan Kahan, a professor of law and psychology at Yale, notes that the more scientifically curious people are, the less partisan they are in their political thinking. In a 2017 paper called 'Science Curiosity and Political Information Processing' (published in the *Advances in Political Psychology* journal), Kahan and his team looked at how people of different levels of political conviction and persuasion responded to questions on 'hot button' topics. (The studies were carried out in the US, so it mostly relates to Democrats and Republicans answering questions on politically charged topics such as global warming.) Kahan found that scientifically curious people (as distinct from knowledge of science – you don't necessarily need to know a lot about science to be scientifically curious) were less likely to answer questions in a partisan manner. Instead, they were more interested in learning about and understanding what was really going on, rather than in seeking out evidence that merely confirmed the prejudices of their political peer group.

More importantly for our purposes, highly intellectually humble people are also better at judging the strength of a persuasive argument and the quality of the evidence behind it than those who are low in intellectual humility. The good news is that you can become more intellectually humble. Here's how.

1. IT'S NOT ABOUT BEING SMARTER THAN THE REST

Beating the market isn't about being cleverer than everyone else, so don't take your success or failure as a judgement of your intellect. No one is cleverer than the market. The market represents the combined brain power of the investment community, and at least a few of those people have higher IQs, better educations, and a lot more resources to throw at the problem than you do. However, there are limits to the value of intelligence in markets. Clever people – like Keynes – tend to assume that they can beat the market through sheer brain power. That's not how it works. As Warren Buffett puts it in the foreword to Benjamin Graham's *The Intelligent Investor*: "To invest successfully does not require a stratospheric IQ, unusual business insights, or inside information. What's needed is a sound intellectual framework for making decisions and the ability to keep emotions from corroding the framework."

2. HAVE YOU EARNED "THE RIGHT TO AN OPINION"?

More important than intellect is understanding the limits of your knowledge – or the extent of your "circle of competence", as Buffett's business partner Charlie Munger puts it. A good way to acknowledge the limits of your understanding is to ask yourself the above question. It's a tip from Ray Dalio, founder of Bridgewater, one of the most successful hedge funds in the world. As we saw in chapter 5, Dalio nearly went bust in 1982 after he correctly predicted that Mexico would default on its debt, but incorrectly expected the market to crash as a result. "It gave me the humility that I needed to become more successful ... I shifted my attitude from thinking: 'I'm right', to asking myself: 'How do I know I'm right?' And that opened my mind a lot." Put simply, it's not just about what you know – it's about understanding what you don't yet know, and what it is you need to know in order to "have the right to an opinion", as Dalio puts it.

In Dalio's case, he was right about the default – but what he lacked enough knowledge on (at the time) was the likely outcome, given historical precedent. If you're convinced of something, ask yourself how you know the view is correct, or even valid – what's your evidence? Question each aspect of your investment thesis – how solid is the reasoning behind it? As you interrogate your investment case, you are quite likely to find that at least some important elements of it are based on assumptions for which you have little or no evidence. You need to plug those gaps. Again, this is hard work – but it's better to find out before you lose money.

3. RENT OPINIONS, DON'T BUY THEM

As we've already seen, one of our biggest problems with seeking out new information and questioning our own ideas is that we don't want to do it. That's the power of confirmation bias – we pay more attention to information that backs up what we already believe. As trading coach Van Tharp puts it, "the more you believe something to be true, the more you will have accumulated evidence to support it." You need only look at social media to see the evidence of this – a recent analysis of groups on Twitter, for example, found that like-minded people followed each other exclusively to the extent that most users are operating in an echo chamber in which they never hear any conflicting or discomfiting opinions.

According to widely quoted advice from Paul Saffo, director of Palo Alto's Institute for the Future, one of the best ways to resist this tendency is to aim to have "strong opinions, which are weakly held". Strong opinions matter, because if you are putting money at risk, you want to do it on the basis of a high-conviction, well-developed argument. But you don't want to get too attached to that opinion, because you'll avoid evidence that contradicts it. That's a particular problem in investment, because even if your view is correct today, it will eventually be incorrect in the future, and at that point, you don't want to be left clinging to it for old times' sake.

4 . GET COMFORTABLE WITH NOT HAVING AN OPINION

A corollary of the last few points is that you don't need to have a view on everything in the market, and you should learn to be comfortable with admitting to this. As writer Nick Romeo put it in a recent essay on behavioural economics and Plato for *Aeon*, "an initial tolerance of uncertainty is a capacity without which individuals and societies cannot adequately self-correct and improve". The main reason to feel relaxed about not having enough knowledge to have an opinion is that if you can't cope with uncertainty you will tend to "reach prematurely for whatever apparent reasons are most accessible" – and as a result jump to the wrong conclusions with an unreasonable level of conviction.

5. BE "ACTIVELY OPEN-MINDED"

How do you avoid getting overly attached to your current set of assumptions? As Jonathan Baron, professor of psychology at University of Pennsylvania, puts it, you have to be "actively open-minded". Force yourself out of your intellectual comfort zone. As Philip Tetlock, the author of *Superforecasting* and an expert in helping individuals to improve their ability to make good forecasts, notes, foxes (people who know a little about a lot) are better at forecasting than hedgehogs (people who have a lot of knowledge within a small field). So read widely and expose yourself to as many different ways of looking at the world as possible.

6. SEEK OUT QUALITY INFORMATION

This doesn't mean just reading any old guff – you don't have endless amounts of time, so you need to learn to filter out what's worth reading and what's going to give you the same old information repackaged. You need to find good sources of information – ones that present you with facts you haven't read elsewhere. They tend not to be sensational (sensationally presented sources can be useful, so do not discount them – but just be aware that they are often merely noisy presentations of an argument made better and more soberly elsewhere). They are often strongly opinionated, but not overly polemical (in other words, they are high-conviction arguments, but not deeply emotionally invested ones). If the writer has a track record of making calls (not all of them do), then examine it. Permabulls and permabears can be useful sources in terms of producing arguments that you have not yet considered yourself, so again, they shouldn't be discounted.

However, an ability to think flexibly and to do so in public is rare, and those who can regularly get both the bearish and the bullish calls right deserve your attention, because it suggests that they are looking at evidence dispassionately, rather than just seeing what they want to see.

For example, there are some people who can legitimately claim to have seen the last financial crisis coming, without necessarily having been permabears (even a stopped clock is right twice a day, after all). But there is a much smaller subset who then also told investors to get back into the market near the bottom in 2009 (Jeremy Grantham of GMO was one, for example). Also, get to understand people's strengths and weaknesses. There are certain pundits who you will grow to realise can be ignored on certain things, but who can be quite informative on others.

Finally, simplicity is a virtue. Finance is a moderately complicated topic, but that doesn't excuse pretentious writing. A good financial writer or analyst should be able to explain pretty much any concept that they themselves understand properly to the average man or woman in the pub. If someone is over-complicating a topic with technical language (where the audience is non-technical), or by citing obscure Greek myths as analogies which, in fact, shed no light on the subject, they are either trying to hide what's really going on (common in the financial industry) or they are struggling to understand the topic themselves (common in the newspaper industry). Find an alternative source.

7. GET ANGRY — BUT UNDERSTAND WHY

Resist your craving to only look at things that support your views, particularly your political views. Put the items you most want to read to the bottom of your reading pile (or your inbox). Instead, pick up the stuff that makes you angry. If a piece is making you angry, it demonstrates two things: a) you are probably too emotionally invested in your own opinion to be able to assess its validity; and b) you feel threatened by the arguments being made in the piece you are reading, which means that you probably don't know enough to counter them. Start by assuming that the person who wrote this piece is roughly as smart as you are, and that they have a similar moral outlook. So why do they disagree with you? Analyse their arguments one by one. Where are you confident that they are wrong? And where are you struggling to challenge their take? Work out where they are able to poke holes in your own views, and then either go out and find evidence to plug those holes, or – painful as it may seem – consider whether you need to revisit your own assumptions.

8. DON'T BE AFRAID TO ADMIT TO BEING WRONG

In the *FT* in 2017, journalist Robin Wigglesworth spoke to William Danoff of Fidelity's giant contrarian Contrafund. Danoff talks about how he started selling out of tech giant Amazon in 2013, because he was concerned about the impact of competition in the cloud computing sector. In the year to the end of 2014, he cut his holding in the group by more than half. However, shares in Amazon kept rising – partly because the company was proving to be very competitive within cloud services – and he ended up buying back in. He'd sold at an average of around $350, and bought back in at around $450, which must have hurt. Yet since then, the share price has more than tripled – so failing to acknowledge his error would have hurt a lot more. As Danoff puts it: "You've got to be flexible, and you've got to be humble, and you've got to be willing to admit mistakes."

9. DON'T GET COCKY

The other danger, of course, and the one that we started this chapter with, is that you get things right. When an investment does well and goes the way you thought it would, it can be a good idea to take a break. If you're feeling euphoric, if you're feeling that you're on a roll, then consider taking your winnings off the table and sitting on them for a while. You've grown used to seeing the world through one lens. Now that the world has changed, your lens will need to change too, and adapting to that takes time, particularly as you will now feel instinctively attached to the viewpoint that has proved profitable for you.

CHAPTER

10

How to Spot Bubbles and What to Do About Them

What are bubbles?

EVEN IF YOU are a complete stranger to the world of investment, you will be familiar with investment bubbles. Tulipomania, the South Sea Bubble, the dotcom boom – they are each epic tales that fit one of the most compelling narrative templates of all – that pride comes before a fall, that blind greed is folly, and that you can't get rich quick. Bubbles typically involve a cast of larger-than-life characters and help to confirm the listener's prejudices about what makes humans and the investment world tick, whatever those may be. They drag normal people in and leave individuals with war stories of fortunes made and fortunes squandered. They're also a point at which particularly bold contrarians can earn bragging rights by avoiding the worst of the excesses, while profiting from the implosion.

Yet despite a wide range of examples from history that most of us can clearly label as bubbles, there is no agreement within the economics profession as to how to identify a bubble market. To understand why, let's take this working definition of a bubble from Markus Brunnermeier of Princeton University, in the *New Palgrave Dictionary of Economics* (2008, 2nd ed):

> "Bubbles are typically associated with dramatic asset price increases followed by a collapse. Bubbles arise if the price exceeds the asset's fundamental value. This can occur if investors hold the asset because

they believe that they can sell it at a higher price to some other investor even though the asset's price exceeds its fundamental value."

While this is a good description, it also gets to the heart of the problem. One of the defining characteristics of a bubble is that it is "followed by a collapse" – in other words, it bursts. Until that happens, you can't say for sure that you're in a bubble. After all, not every asset that enjoys rapid price gains is in a bubble – sometimes prices go up and stay there. As William N. Goetzmann of Yale School of Management sums it up: "Bubbles are booms that went bad."

Why should you care?

From an investor's point of view, what's interesting about bubbles is that they make a lot of money on the way up, then lose it all on the way down. So in an ideal world, you'd be able to spot the assets that have bubble potential, ride them all the way up, and then identify the warning signs that allow you to get out at or near the top.

On that front, I've got some bad news for you – no one can do that. No one can reliably figure out which assets will end up in bubble territory, and even once they've reached bubble territory, you can't then reliably tell when the bubble is going to burst.

So why are we even talking about them? Because at some point in your investment life – and probably more than once – you will be caught up in a bubble and you will get caught up in a bust. Having some understanding of what's going on could place you in a position to profit, or to at least help you to avoid making the most destructive errors.

What you need to know about bubbles

One big risk – particularly for those who consider themselves contrarians – is to be too keen to shout 'bubble!'. The fact is that bubbles are rare. And even what seems like an obvious bubble can go on for literally years after it has first been spotted. When then-Federal Reserve chairman Alan Greenspan warned of "irrational exuberance" in the stock market on 5 December 1996, the dotcom bubble had barely started. The tech-heavy Nasdaq index almost quadrupled between then and its peak in March 2000. And while the Nasdaq did eventually shed all of those gains, it only ever touched Greenspan's warning level again briefly at the tail end of the tech crash, and then again after the 2008 financial crisis. In short, Greenspan's warning was of no real informational value to an investor. In all likelihood, if you had been invested in the Nasdaq, and you then bailed out on the Fed boss's words, you'd have nursed a strong case of sellers' regret and almost certainly got back in at the worst possible time.

The key point to understand about bubbles is that they are about extremes. Regardless of how much you know about your financial history, their sheer ability to keep going beyond the apparent point of rationality will take you by surprise, which is what makes them so difficult to navigate.

Extreme overvaluation

A key concept underlying our understanding of bubbles and busts is the idea of 'mean reversion'. This is basically just the observation that markets have their ups and downs. Sometimes they'll be close to their 'fundamental' value (which is typically derived from the future cash flows the asset is expected to generate) and sometimes they'll be far away from it (either above or below it). You can imagine mean reversion as being a piece of elastic that ties the asset's price to its fundamental value. If the elastic gets too stretched in one direction or another, it'll eventually ping back, and probably overshoot in the opposite direction as it does. Not everything reverts to the mean, and mean reversion can take a long time, but it's a very useful rule of thumb.

For an asset to be in genuine bubble territory – as Brunnermeier's definition implies – it needs to be overvalued. And not just a little bit overvalued – it has to be egregiously so. Indeed, as far as hedge fund manager Cliff Asness of AQR Capital Management is concerned: "To have content, the term 'bubble' should indicate a price that no reasonable future outcome can justify. I believe that tech stocks in early 2000 fit this description. I don't think there were assumptions – short of them owning the GDP of the Earth – that justified their valuations."[2] Those are the sorts of valuations we're talking about – ones that, when viewed in the cold light of day, are scarcely believable.

To get more technical about it, US asset manager GMO – which has studied more bubbles than most – settled on a definition that views an asset as having entered bubble territory

2   www.cfapubs.org/doi/pdf/10.2469/faj.v70.n1.2

when it is valued at two or more standard deviations away from its long-term trend. Standard deviation sounds complicated, but it's just a statistical measure – a two-standard-deviation event is mathematically improbable (it should only happen once every 44 years) so if an asset price hits this level, it means it is well out of whack with its normal range, suggesting that reversion is overdue. GMO reckons that of 35 major market moves that it defined as bubbles under this definition (as of 2011), 33 went on to see a bust that wiped out all of the bubble-era gains. Examples include the dotcom bubble, the 2008 US housing bubble, and the Japanese equity (and commercial property) bubbles of the 1980s.

The other key ingredient: extreme enthusiasm

But as GMO's own Jeremy Grantham points out, you can't rely solely on valuations. Based on many valuation measures (notably the cyclically-adjusted P/E ratio, or Cape, which we'll look at in more detail in the next chapter), for example, the US stock market has been relatively expensive for most of the time since the rally began in 2009, and yet it has enjoyed a lengthy bull market. So while valuation can confirm for you that a market is expensive, it can't tell you when it has gone over the edge into the unquestioning bullish hysteria that a proper bubble requires. A very expensive asset can carry on getting even more expensive for much longer than you might think; or as hedge fund manager David Einhorn once put it in the *Financial Times*, "twice a silly price is not twice as silly; it's still just silly." That means that you need to keep an eye on sentiment – what Grantham calls "the touchy-feely stuff". And for that you need to have an idea of how a bubble's storyline evolves.

The story of a typical bubble

A bubble always starts off as eminently rational. Indeed, it usually starts with a contrarian idea that ends up going mainstream. And most bubbles follow a loosely similar storyline – the price charts of history's greatest bubbles resemble each other surprisingly closely. Here are some of the key stages to look out for.

- **Recognition of huge potential:** a truly epic bubble is built in layers. They are often fuelled by the rise of a transformative new technology, such as the internet or the railways, or a major demographic or political shift suddenly opening up huge opportunities for investment (postwar Japan, or China's opening up to globalisation, for example). In short, as GMO's Grantham puts it, "there's never been a bubble when the fundamentals did not shine."[3] New financial technology often plays a role, too – anything that makes it easier to get credit, or that reduces the frictional costs of transacting, or that opens up new markets, can encourage the flows of money towards a boom asset. It also helps – as financial historian Edward Chancellor noted, also in a piece for GMO – if there is "no valuation anchor". You want a situation with such vast potential that almost no valuation can be dismissed as categorically

3 pro.creditwritedowns.com/2018/01/grantham-bubble-wonderful-fundamentals-euphorically-extrapolated.html

absurd, and investors can let their imaginations run wild. Tech stocks were a good example, as is the more recent frenzy for cryptocurrencies.

- **A damn good story:** these sound fundamentals are recognised by a smart group of early investors. Other investors start to notice prices rising and get behind the theme. They get in, and the word gets out. What early investors recognised as exciting fundamentals are boiled down into a hot story, one that is simple to understand and easy to spread. So 'the Chinese population is increasingly moving from the countryside to the cities and the government is embarking on a massive roadbuilding programme, so it will require a lot more raw materials' turns into 'imagine if everyone in China owned two cars and a fridge-freezer!'.

- **Satire and establishment sneers:** there's a persistent myth that people don't see bubbles coming, but the truth is that there are sceptical voices almost all the way through any bubble. The establishment dislikes change – change is hard work – and so mainstream opinion columnists usually prefer, initially, to dismiss the new era than attempt to wrap their heads around it. (Paul Krugman, Nobel-Prize-winning economist, famously predicted – not entirely seriously, to be fair – in a 1998 piece for *Time* that "by 2005 or so, it will become clear that the internet's impact on the economy has been no greater than the fax machine's."). And one of the main reasons we know about the tulip bubble at all is from satirical pamphlets written during the period (some argue that these have contributed to an exaggerated view of how extensive the bubble was). Indeed, satire is worth watching out for – it's a sign that a trend is embedded firmly enough in the popular consciousness to be worth satirising. One of the most famous examples of South Sea mania, sometimes quoted in seriousness, was a satirical proposal to launch "a company for carrying on an undertaking of great advantage, but nobody to know what it is". And the cryptocurrency mania took it to newly self-referential levels – a joke currency based on a meme, Dogecoin, briefly became one of the most valuable cryptocurrencies on the market.

- **Rationalising away the uncomfortable reality:** those who missed out on the early stages see the gains mount and grow keen to get onboard. Genuinely valid critiques of the thesis behind the bubble (as opposed to knee-jerk reactions by people who can't be bothered to understand what's going on) are crowded out as bigger institutions start to buy in, and give the bullish story another aggressive push, frequently backed by official-looking forecasts based on cherry-picked data, barely supportable assumptions, and blue-sky extrapolations. By this point, the price has long since eclipsed the fundamentals, but rather than sell out, investors rationalise the gains by throwing out the old measurements, saying that they no longer work and finding new ones that do.

So a cyclical commodities boom becomes a never-ending 'supercycle'; an oil boom is the result of oil running out ('peak oil'); and companies with no earnings or profits are deemed to have value based on the number of people clicking on their website. Thus it becomes a self-reinforcing process – rising prices encourage investors to seek new arguments to rationalise them, and these arguments are then used to justify prices rising further. Eye-catching price targets are something to watch out for at this stage – Dow 36,000! $200 oil! $100,000 bitcoin! It's also around about this point that the same opinion columnists who sneered in the early days start to fall in line with the 'new paradigm' arguments.

- **Increasingly unstable financing:** towards the later stages of the bubble, leverage – borrowed money – becomes increasingly vital to keep the show on the road. Lenders are keen to get exposure to the sector, and those who missed out on the early stages hope to play catch-up by using borrowed money to boost their profits – so money keeps flowing into the market, which keeps going higher as a result. Economist Hyman Minsky noted that what he described as "Ponzi borrowing" – lending that can only be repaid as long as asset prices keep rising – becomes the dominant form of finance.

The tipping point – spotting the top of the market

By this point, the underlying structure is based on such flimsy foundations that pretty much anything can knock it over. This is why, if you look at the classic bubbles throughout history, it's very rarely possible to say exactly what brought them to an end. It's like an avalanche. The proximate cause could be the gust of wind that toppled the pebble that set the whole thing cascading down the mountain. But the reason for the avalanche is not the wind or the pebble – it's the fundamental structural instability, built up over a period of years or even decades.

However, certain factors do tend to be present when a bubble bursts. Here are a few major red flags to watch out for.

- **Rising interest rates:** the formation of asset bubbles is almost always aided and abetted by the availability of cheap money. In turn, they burst when the cheap money dries up. So while it doesn't happen overnight, a rising interest rate environment is something to watch out for. For example, the Federal Reserve started raising interest rates in 1998, and didn't lower them again until 2001. Similarly, the Fed raised interest rates in mid-2004 and didn't lower them again until late 2007, at which point it was clear that the US housing bubble had burst.

- **An acceleration, or 'melt-up':** as Gavyn Davies of Fulcrum Asset Management notes, one factor distinguishing bubbles from booms is that the market gets far ahead of itself – experiencing "explosive growth in equity prices adjusted for fundamentals". This tends to be accentuated in the final stages, as those who haven't yet piled into the market throw the towel in and are gripped by fear of missing out (FOMO), rather than fear of losing money. This 'get me in at any cost' mentality is what drives the frenzied final throes of a bubble market. Grantham's analysis of bubbles suggests that this 'melt-up' phase typically lasts for around 21 months and sees a gain of at least 60%.

- **Deteriorating fundamentals, reluctant bulls, capitulating bears, and running on faith:** readers of a certain age will remember the Road Runner cartoons, in which the Road Runner's hapless would-be nemesis Wile E. Coyote would regularly run off the side of a cliff and then keep going, only succumbing to gravity when the Road Runner pointed out that he was running on thin air. The tail end of bubble markets is often a case of waiting for the market's Wile E. Coyote moment. The fundamentals are often clearly deteriorating (banks going bust as in 2008, companies burning cash with nothing to show for it as in the 2000s, the economy slowing down and interest rates rising), yet no one wants to leave the party first because they've seen too many early bears ruin their careers.

So look out for a sense of complacent resignation and cynicism among professional investors, who struggle to argue the case for further gains (or talk about 'cash on the sidelines' or 'walls of money' from sovereign wealth funds or other non-existent potential benefactors who might keep things ticking over) but equally can't see any alternative, particularly when a crash would be bad for their own business. Also look out for previously bearish pundits throwing in the towel and admitting defeat. These new converts will embrace the bubble with the conviction and relief of those who have finally seen the light in the face of adversity – a form of market Stockholm syndrome – generally just in time to see it pop.

- **Mammoth M&A deals and IPOs:** what is the easiest time to sell a bubble asset? At the height of the bubble, of course. And it's fair to say that CEOs have an almost uncanny ability to call the top of the market. In January 2000, less than three months before the tech bubble peaked, internet pioneer AOL bought old media giant Time Warner in the biggest merger deal ever up to that point. In 2007, RBS and Barclays banking executives warred over the right to buy Dutch rival ABN Amro. RBS secured the deal in October 2007 – the same month that stocks peaked – and partly as a result, at the time of writing, it is still owned by the UK taxpayer while Barclays managed to squeak its way through the financial crisis while remaining in private hands. And in May 2011, privately-held Glencore, the largest commodities trading house in the world, went public in the largest ever international IPO seen on the London market. That same month, the Bloomberg commodity index (an index composed of commodities from energy to agriculture to industrial and precious metals) hit its post-2008 rally peak. Again this is qualitative rather than quantitative – you can't explicitly say that 'a deal of this size will be done, indicating the top' – but when you combine a headline-grabbing deal with an overvalued market it's a pretty decent indicator of a turning point.

- **Extraordinary statistics and things that make no sense:** similar to headline-grabbing deals, you will often see statistics that are simply astonishing. Famous examples include the following: in 1989, the land under the Emperor's Palace in Japan (roughly 3.5 square kilometres of prime Tokyo real estate) was thought to be worth the same as all the real estate in the state of California put together.[4] At the peak of the tech bubble, in March 2000, notes Bank of America Merrill Lynch, the market capitalisation of Yahoo alone was 25 times that of the entire Chinese stock market. More recently, in signs that could well mark the end of the lengthy bond bull market, in summer 2016 the Swiss government was able to borrow money over a 50-year period at a

---

4 amaral.northwestern.edu/blog/how-much-was-japanese-imperial-palace-worth

negative interest rate – in other words, demand for safe assets was so high that investors were willing to pay to own them.

How to deal with bubbles

Dealing with bubbles – as with many things in investment – is mainly a case of managing your instinctive reactions. As Howard Marks of Oaktree Capital puts it, bubbles might be triggered by fundamentals, but they are "pushed to their extremes by swings in emotion". So the best thing you can do is to avoid being pushed about by the same emotions as everyone else. If you don't, then "your behaviour will be typical: pro-cyclical and painfully wrong at the extremes." The reason that bubbles and busts do so much damage to people's capital is because investors panic at the wrong time. They get in at the top (because they can't bear the market going up without them) and they get out at the bottom (because they can't bear the losses anymore). How do you avoid that?

- **It's OK to sit a bubble out:** the first thing to remember is: you don't have to participate. A lot of money can be made in bubbles, so it's nice to ride them up. But if you've missed a boom, then the worst thing you can do is try to play catch-up. For the majority of today's investors, the most salient example of a bubble bursting is the crash of 2008, which was so widespread that it was very difficult to hide from. But most bubbles are not quite so far-reaching. You didn't have to own Japan in the 1980s, you didn't have to own tech stocks in the 1990s, and you could have opted out of the commodities bubble in the 2000s. Also, micro-bubbles come and go all the time. You missed the lithium bubble? The 3D printing bubble? Who cares? Another overhyped sector will be along shortly. Remember – your big advantage is that you don't suffer from career risk – no one is judging you on next quarter's figures. So it doesn't matter that your neighbour made 30% in tech stocks, 100% in buy-to-let, or 1,032% in cryptocurrencies last year. Good for him. Park your frustration and your envy and accept that unless your own hard-headed analysis leads you to believe that the sector still represents a big opportunity, then there's no reason for you to follow him in.

- **Shorting is tempting but inadvisable:** opting out of the bubble altogether can feel like a bit of a cop-out. If you've been smart enough to identify it, why not profit from your foresight by short selling the bubble assets? The Templeton tech-bubble bet we noted in chapter 8 is a beautiful example of a well-executed short. Templeton knew the market was overvalued and he also identified a catalyst in the form of share lock-ups expiring. However, there are a few very good practical reasons – particularly for private investors – to avoid shorting. Firstly, short selling exposes you to theoretically unlimited losses. A share price can only fall by 100%, but it can rise indefinitely. Secondly, shorting usually involves using leverage (borrowed money), which makes the process even riskier – there's a high chance of being stopped out of your position in the short run, even if your investment view turns out to be right in the longer run. So you can lose many multiples of your original stake. I'm not saying that it can't be done successfully, but shorting is not a buy-and-hold strategy. It's a high-risk trading strategy, and one that is beyond the scope of this book. It requires an extremely tight focus on managing risk, along with the mastery of a very different set of tools (chart-reading skills for one) if you want to have any hope of making a profit. So unless you are wedded to the idea, I would avoid directly shorting the market.

- **Look out for anti-bubble opportunities:** an alternative to shorting is to look for anti-bubble assets that are likely to benefit once the current trend changes. Typically, if one asset or sector is in a rampant bull market, you'll find another that's been neglected. Just as the tech bubble was bursting in 2000, for example, the boom in 'real' assets – commodities and property – was ready to get going. And one of the hottest sectors in the post-2009 rally was the one that had been hated for years by investors who were badly burned by the 2000 bust – tech stocks.

- **Protect your profits:** let's say you are already on board – you spotted the opportunity early when the current bubble asset was still cheap, you've made a lot of money, but now you're getting jittery. There are two main options, both of which require discipline. One is that you set a stop-loss. You decide on a price point, or a percentage loss, at which you accept the bubble is over and the bust has begun. This relies on a couple of things – you have to have got in early enough to have profits worth protecting; and you must find a strategy that you'll stick to. One big problem with bubbles is that smart people get out too early, watch it carry on up without them, and then vaporise all of their profits in increasingly desperate attempts to get back what they lost by missing the top.

So find a sensible way of setting a target that allows you to trump your own instincts. If you like charts, you could use a moving average strategy to indicate a change of trend, or you could simply set a trailing stop-loss (e.g. you'll sell once the market falls 20% from its most recent high). You won't sell at the top but you will get out before the bottom (which in proper bubbles, remember, is often 80% or so away from the top). However, the most important thing is that once you're out, you stay out – don't second guess yourself, as that way lies profit destruction. Draw a line under the experience and move on.

An alternative, simple strategy is simply to rebalance. We'll look at that in more detail in chapter 15, but it basically means reducing your exposure without being entirely out of the market.

The best feature about bubbles

The best thing (for a sceptical investor) about bubbles is that they create busts, and busts create cracking opportunities. Bubbles are arguably more psychologically difficult than busts because there is a huge fear of missing out. You can never have enough money invested in a bubble market – even if you are participating, you will always be thinking: 'Why didn't I invest more?' And that sort of thinking is painful. Busts, on the other hand, play to a sceptical investor's key strength – patience, and the ability to keep your head while everyone around you is losing theirs.

- **Don't panic:** the popping of a bubble is a little like the 'reveal' in a horror film. At first there's a mild sense of unease. A few hedge funds go bust, an IPO fails to take off. There's a burst of panic, often followed by a false dawn. ('Was that it? Does the bailout of Northern Rock draw a line under this?') And then the carnage begins. The process of discovering just how much rubbish was swept under the carpet during the boom is dramatic and painful. Every day the news just seems to get worse and worse. The speed of the deterioration is also shocking – as the old saying goes, 'Bull markets take the stairs, a bear market comes down in the lift.'

- **Know your portfolio inside out:** this is the point at which you really need to understand what's in your portfolio and why it's there. Assuming that you are not hanging on to the assets at the epicentre of the bubble, the falling price is not a good reason to sell what you believe is a good quality asset. Amid the general sense of panic, and the occasional sea of red on your portfolio statement, that's not always easy to remember. But just as the general sense of euphoria should not have driven your decision to invest in an asset, nor should the general sense of panic drive you out of it.

- **Look out for buying opportunities:** just as you can't call the top, there's no easy way to spot the bottom of a market either. But in many ways, it's the mirror image of a bubble. First, there's valuation – the market gets cheap, or at least much closer to fair value, on various historically reliable measures. Second, there's sentiment – just as investors become irrationally optimistic on the way up, they become wildly pessimistic on the way down, until they are eventually pricing in far too much potential bad news. As we noted at the start of chapter 7, the time to buy is typically not when things get better – it's when they stop getting worse.

However, the big difference between the bubble phase and the bust is that timing becomes less important. Bailing out of a bubble market too early can be extraordinarily frustrating. An undervalued market can fall a lot further and for a lot longer than you might expect. But if you start feeding money in when – and only when – you are confident that it's cheap, then in the longer run, history shows that you'll make money. The key, of course, is that word 'cheap' – and in the next chapter, we'll look at some ways to measure that.

CHAPTER

11

Finding the World's Cheapest Markets

FOLLOWING ON FROM the last chapter – if we agree that the best opportunities are to be found when markets are cheap, then what's the best way to hunt down global stock markets that are cheap compared to their history?

There are many ways to measure stock market valuations, but one of the most popular is the cyclically-adjusted price/earnings (CAPE) ratio, also known as the Shiller P/E ratio, after Professor Robert Shiller, who popularised it. The CAPE takes the average of the last ten years' worth of market earnings and compares it with the current market value (rather than using one year's worth of earnings, as with a traditional P/E ratio). The idea behind taking average earnings over a decade is to account for fluctuations in the business cycle – depending on the state of the economy at a given time, a company's annual earnings might be unusually high or unusually low (particularly for cyclical companies such as house builders or miners, who can go from peak earnings to huge losses in the course of a year when the market turns against them). So taking the average over ten years means you smooth out these ups and downs and can get a better picture of whether or not a market is expensive relative to its long-term average earnings.

Using data going back to 1871, Shiller split the US market into quintiles according to CAPE value. He calculated that if investors bought in at times when the CAPE was in its lowest quintile, future returns tended to be high, and when the CAPE was in its highest quintile, future returns tended to be low. So over time, if you buy the market when you can get £1-worth of ten-year average earnings for £10 or so, or even less – then history suggests that you are likely to make more money in the long term than if you buy when the CAPE is high – say, when you're paying £20 or even £30 for £1 of ten-year average earnings. In short, buying when stocks are cheap beats buying when they're expensive. So the CAPE can highlight good long-term buying opportunities.

Criticisms of the CAPE

Now, the CAPE has come in for a fair bit of criticism during the post-2009 bull market. This is largely because if you had used a strict version of the CAPE you might never have invested at the bottom of the US market in 2009 (the market only fell to fair value, not generational lows) and even if you had, the market rapidly became overvalued on a CAPE basis. As a result, various commentators have come forward with their objections to the CAPE – they say it is overly conservative because the average earnings component is dragged lower by a horrendously bad year such as 2008 (which in turn pushes the CAPE higher than it otherwise would be), or they argue that accounting standards have changed, or that there are reasons – such as the dawn of the internet – why stocks should now trade at permanently higher P/E ratios.

However, while some of these complaints are more valid than others, none of them deals a true killer blow to the CAPE. For a start, the CAPE is not an outlier – it's far from the only measure that suggests that US markets in the mid-to-late 2010s have been consistently expensive. The Warren Buffett indicator (so-called because Buffett described it to *Fortune* magazine in 2001 as being "probably the best single measure of where valuations stand at any given moment") compares market capitalisation to GDP, on the basis that the stock market can't realistically grow faster than the underlying economy for very long. Like the CAPE it has been at very elevated levels. Same goes for Tobin's Q (a measure of the replacement value – the book value – of the market compared to the actual price of the market). The idea with Tobin's Q is that if you can set a company up from scratch for less than it would cost you to buy it outright on the market, it means the market is overvalued. All of these measures and more have been telling a similar story to the CAPE – so it's not unusually out of line with other measures.

More to the point, we know that while the CAPE is a decent indicator, there are no guarantees that individual markets will always follow the pattern. Indeed, as Mebane Faber of Cambria Investment Management points out, if you take the CAPE and apply it to the performance of global markets in recent years, the US itself is actually something of an outlier – it's pretty much the only highly expensive market that continued to deliver strong returns; the exception that proves the rule if you will.

In any case, from a sceptical investor's point of view, as we discussed in chapter 10, finding the markets that are overvalued is arguably of less interest than finding the ones that are undervalued. What's more important is that the CAPE gives a very strong indication of when a market is cheap, because it's mainly the cheap markets that we want to identify in the first instance – because these are the ones that we actually want to invest in.

The results you get by buying at generational lows

The CAPE has mostly been used to study the US stock market, which – alongside the UK market – has the longest run of data available. However, while most international markets have smaller data sets, the CAPE has been shown to be effective in most overseas markets too. In the 2014 edition of his book, *Global Value*, Faber looked at all the occasions where a market's CAPE had hit rock bottom – i.e. fallen below seven – since 1980. He and his team found just 28 instances of these generational lows out of more than 800 market years he studied in total.

This is not unusual, by the way. Financial historian Russell Napier looked at periods when the CAPE had fallen to exceptionally low levels in his forensic analysis of the best times in the last century to buy the US market, *Anatomy of the Bear: Lessons from Wall Street's Four Great Bottoms*. There were really only three occasions in a century in which the US market fell that low on a CAPE valuation basis (those times were 1921, 1932 and 1982 – at the bottom in 1949, the other 'great bear', the CAPE had only fallen to around 11).

So what did Faber find? If you had bought global stock markets consistently when the CAPE was sitting at below seven, then on average you made more than 30% in the following year alone, and an annualised return of 14.4% over the following decade – an exceptionally good return, roughly twice what pension funds (not known for their pessimism) assume you'll make from equities in the long run. As Faber puts it: "Historically, investors have been rewarded for taking the risk of buying countries with extremely low valuations." Meanwhile, if you bought when CAPE was at extreme highs – 45 and above – you typically lost nearly 9% in the following year, and made a very weak 1.2% a year over the next decade. It also typically took an overpriced market around three and a half years to get back to 'fair value' (defined by Faber as a CAPE below 17).

So what does it take to drive markets to those sorts of bargain-basement levels? As you might be able to guess, the answer is 'a great deal of bad news'. These are never markets where it looks like a good idea to buy – because if it did, valuations wouldn't be so low. Markets that get to these levels are almost like bubbles turned upside down – just as a bubble starts with good fundamentals taken to extremes, a bust like this starts with awful fundamentals taken to extremes. It almost requires a scenario whereby investors can believe that, in the worst case, no price is too low – we're talking about Greece during the points in the eurozone crisis when it was only ever one more last-ditch meeting away from being kicked out of the eurozone for good. We're talking about Russia when relationships with the West have been at their worst and talk of sanctions and war are in the headlines.

In short, for markets to be this cheap, it has to feel like you'd be mad to touch them with a ten-foot bargepole. And yet, as the old contrarian cliché about 'buying when there's blood in the streets' has it, these are the times to buy.

How to take advantage
without over-exposing yourself

Situations like the above are rare, as Faber's research suggests. Most of the time, you don't see these extremes. But markets don't have to be in dire straits to be worth buying. You can still make decent money by investing in inexpensive markets as opposed to those on the edge of Armageddon. Faber suggests that one good way to use the CAPE is to find the cheapest 25% of global markets each year, and to invest in them (you rebalance each year – you roll the money over into the current 25% cheapest markets). How would that have done historically? Well, there's limited data, but one piece of research by Faber notes that between 1993 and 2015, an investor who had put 100% of their money in the S&P 500 would have made just over 780% (around 9% a year). That's a decent return, especially given that it's during a period in which the CAPE on the US market was either above average or expensive for pretty much the entire time, bar a few months during the financial crisis. However, if you had moved your money into the cheapest global markets by CAPE each year, then you'd have made an impressive 2,520% over the same period – that's 14.5% a year – soundly thrashing the US market option.

That's all very well, but it may sound impractical to invest in the likes of Russia or Portugal or Italy. Yet the good news is that exchange-traded funds (ETFs) make it easy. These days, it's fair to say that almost regardless of how obscure the market is, you can find an ETF that represents it. The indices used by Faber are the ones used by index provider MSCI rather than the headline indices for each country (e.g. rather than the FTSE 100 or All-

Share, it's the MSCI UK index), and you'll find relatively cheap ETF options for most of the countries involved – potentially not London-listed (if you want to buy a Greek ETF, for example, you'll have to go via the French stock exchange), but generally easily accessible from most stockbrokers. For up-to-date CAPE ratios, Star Capital (starcapital.de) maintains a very useful website that ranks stock markets in terms of value, based on various measures, including the CAPE.

Two key risks: war and communism

The beauty of this strategy is that you are dealing in broad markets, rather than individual stocks. It's rare (although not impossible, as we'll see in a moment) in peacetime for an entire market to go to zero, so it's a way to avoid taking individual company risk. You're also investing using mainstream financial instruments that are priced in real time, so you are minimising fraud risk too.

That said, it's worth being aware of a few things. Buying cheap, good value assets and avoiding expensive ones does make intuitive sense, but past performance is no guide to future performance – you don't know that this strategy will keep paying off just because it did in the past.

Another point is that you do have to buy cheap. It's rare for every market in the world to be overvalued but if stocks in general are in a bull market then it's quite possible that many markets will at least be uninspiring in terms of value, if not grossly overpriced. So even buying cheap markets in that situation will not necessarily protect you from a crash on a given year. In Faber's own backtests, he suggested that you shouldn't be in a market if the CAPE is above 19, even if it's in the cheapest quartile.

Other issues to be aware of include currency risk – any time you buy a financial instrument denominated in another currency, there's the danger that your home currency will strengthen against it and thus reduce your return or amplify your losses. It's something to be aware of in choosing your asset allocation – how much exposure do you want outside your home country?

More specifically, if you're looking at investing in countries that are priced for the apocalypse, it's worth knowing what the worst-case scenario is. Looking back through history, there are a few things that can send a stock market to zero.

Financial historian Russell Napier summed it up in a presentation to the CFA Institute a few years ago. "Always buy equities when the CAPE is lower than ten, with three exceptions: when you believe in communism or fascism and there are no property rights; when you suspect your capital stock can be destroyed by war; or if your currency has entered a new currency regime with an overvalued exchange rate like Greece in the eurozone."

Napier's warning is well founded. Going back through the countries listed in the *Credit Suisse Global Investment Returns Yearbook*, which is updated every year by Elroy Dimson, Paul Marsh and Mike Staunton, the most striking examples of stock markets going to zero are due to communist regimes taking over ("domestic investors in China and Russia effectively lost everything" – Russia in 1917 and China in 1949). But war, clearly, has the potential to be just as devastating – Germany saw its equity market drop in value by 88% during the second world war and its aftermath – and that's without considering the impact of other events that often accompany war, such as hyperinflation or the collapse of legal structures to protect and enforce property rights. In effect, it's all about the destruction or confiscation of capital – cases where your assets might literally be reduced to rubble, or be stolen from you by the state, or both.

These concerns over governance and stability are one reason why emerging markets tend to trade at a discount to developed ones generally (in other words, they tend to have lower CAPEs). More specifically, a country under constant threat of war or structural upheaval, such as South Korea (where reunification would only be slightly less disruptive than war with its northern neighbour) will almost always be a bit cheaper than its peers. The same goes for countries where investors are particularly concerned about the government's commitment to property rights and its propensity for confiscating assets (such as Russia). Capital controls – laws or other government impositions that prevent or limit the flow of money in or out of a country – are a lesser risk but still a genuine one, particularly if you invest your money overseas in a nation that is struggling economically and politically. You might not consider that a problem, depending on the country – as Napier put it at the *MoneyWeek* Conference in 2016: "If your capital is stuck in Italy, I can't think of a better place to spend it" – but overall, I think most of us would like our money to come to us, rather than the other way around. This is why you should diversify.

Overall, investing using the CAPE is a simple, straightforward contrarian strategy which doesn't require too much deep analysis, makes intuitive sense, and has a recent history of good results. It just requires that you have the guts to buy on the odd occasion when all looks lost, without second-guessing the politics of it all – which is something we'll take a look at in more detail in the next chapter.

CHAPTER

12

The Dangerous Temptation of Making Better Forecasts

"P EOPLE IN THIS country have had enough of experts."
Conservative politician Michael Gove's comment during
the European Union referendum campaign has become infamous.
It is in fact a truncated quote – "I think the people of this country
have had enough of experts from organisations with acronyms
saying that they know what is best and getting it consistently
wrong", and is usually misquoted in a critical manner as evidence
of poor thinking on the behalf of those who voted Leave.

Yet, misquoted or not, Gove had a point. Forecasts – from
experts or otherwise – are rarely worth the paper they're printed
on. In his 2005 book, *Expert Political Judgement: How good is
it? How can we know?*, Philip Tetlock writes about how he and
his colleagues conducted a series of forecasting tournaments
between 1984 and 2003, collating 28,000 predictions from 284
experts in fields associated with aggressive, headline-grabbing
prognostications – among them, political scientists, economists
and journalists. They found that the average expert was barely
better than a random guess. "When we pit experts against
minimalist performance benchmarks – dilettantes, dart-throwing
chimps, and assorted extrapolation algorithms – we find few
signs that expertise translates into greater ability to make either
'well-calibrated' or 'discriminating' forecasts."

But what if you could find a way to make better forecasts? If
you could have predicted the results of the US election or the

Brexit referendum accurately, for example, then wouldn't that give you a significant investment edge?

How to make better predictions

We'll return to that latter question further down. But it is certainly possible to become a better forecaster. In his 2015 book *Superforecasters* (written with journalist Dan Gardner), Tetlock explains that despite his apparently disappointing overall results, he did find that a small proportion of people were able consistently to make better predictions than average. Better yet, these superforecasters' techniques could be improved with training. You can read the full story in Tetlock's book, and the Good Judgment Project website (launched by Tetlock and his wife Barbara Mellers) has plenty of training exercises that you can use to hone your own forecasting abilities – if you have time to do so, I'd recommend it.

But in terms of helping us to process the sorts of predictions that investors are faced with every day in the media, and from brokers and fund managers, Tetlock's view of the qualities of a good forecast is particularly useful.

I. A GOOD FORECAST SHOULD BE SPECIFIC, MEASURABLE AND UNAMBIGUOUS

Most expert forecasts in the public domain – and many that aren't – are not specific enough. They don't specify a timescale in which the event should occur, or they leave the wording open to interpretation. This leaves the forecaster with an easy get-out clause if their view apparently fails to come true. It also makes it impossible to measure the quality of the forecast in a systematic way, and thus to measure the track record of the forecaster. So a genuinely useful forecast will have specific parameters against which it can be judged. Say a pundit says that 'inflation is set to take off'. That's not specific enough. How far will it rise? By what date? And how confident are they in the forecast – is it 60% likely to happen? 80%? Forecasts that lack this sort of specificity are not forecasts. They may be useful as big picture what-if scenarios to encourage further thought (along the lines of 'artificial intelligence will take all our jobs'-style predictions), or they may simply be about grabbing headlines for the individual or institution making them. But they're not useful forecasts.

2. THE BEST FORECASTERS MAKE THE WORST TV

One finding from Tetlock's study, he writes in *Superforecasters*, was that it "revealed an inverse correlation between fame and accuracy: the more famous an expert was, the less accurate he was." There was a very simple explanation for this. Tetlock loosely categorises thinkers on a spectrum with "hedgehogs" at one end and "foxes" at the other. The labels are inspired by an essay written by the philosopher Isaiah Berlin, who in turn used a line from ancient Greek: "The fox knows many things but the hedgehog knows one big thing."

The famous forecasters are very much "hedgehog" thinkers. They have "one Big Idea" and they view every problem through the prism of that Big Idea – they are highly ideological. The media in general, and broadcast media in particular, has little tolerance for nuance, which makes "hedgehogs" the ideal thinkers for TV – they have both the ability and the desire to put across simple arguments with conviction. In effect, they start with the conclusion they want to see and then work back from that.

"Foxes", on the other hand, lack the conviction of the "hedgehogs" and thus will tend to make more nuanced, rounded arguments that pull together and consider information from many different sources, rather than only those that agree with their point of view. As Tetlock notes, those traits make for better forecasts, but they don't make for good TV. So while you might enjoy watching or reading the work of your favourite pundits, don't take it too seriously, and always be aware of their "Big Idea", be it environmentalism, low taxation or just a desire to get back at a much-despised rival intellectual.

3. GOOD FORECASTS START FROM THE OUTSIDE, NOT THE INSIDE VIEW

In his book, *Thinking, Fast and Slow*, behavioural psychology pioneer Daniel Kahneman talks about his own experience of making forecasts. He had put together a team to create an academic curriculum and write a textbook for a proposed course on decision-making. One afternoon, reasonably early in the process, he and the team members each individually estimated how long they thought it would take them to finish the course. They came to an average conclusion of around two years. Then Kahneman asked one team member (whose estimate had fallen within a similar range to the rest) about what sort of time it had taken similar groups to complete similar projects. The man somewhat sheepishly realised that he had never seen a curriculum set up from scratch in less than seven years, and that nearly half of such efforts failed along the way. (In the end, the project took eight years, and Kahneman had long since left the team by the time it was finished.)

Kahneman and his research partner, Amos Tversky, described these two different starting points for making forecasts as the "inside view" and the "outside view". The inside view starts with a focus on the specifics of the situation you are trying to analyse. That may seem to make sense – after all, you have the best understanding of your own circumstances. However, in the absence of any neutral reference point to use to calibrate your forecast, the temptation is to focus on the details that back up the case that you want to make, rather than try to produce as dispassionate a judgement as possible. As Michael Mauboussin puts it, "the inside view tends to lead to conclusions that are too optimistic." Instead, start with the "outside view" – rather than focus on the specifics of a single case, look at what 'normally' happens in similar situations. This gives you a "base rate" – a sense of the typical outcome. Only then should you consider whether there are any reasons to expect your specific case to be different.

Brexit, Trump and other political surprises

The idea of becoming a superforecaster is very tempting – contrarians often have a tendency to see themselves as smarter than the average investor, and the idea that you can use your crystal ball to gain an edge is appealing.

And I'd agree that applying a Tetlock-style rigour to your thought process is a good idea. The practice of setting parameters, contemplating different outcomes, and laying it all out in black and white will help you to spot flaws in your thought processes. It will also enable you to tell the difference between a forecast that has value, and mere page-filling pontification – which will add greatly to your understanding of just how flawed and poorly constructed most of the public predictions we see from opinionated columnists, attention-seeking theorists, and media-friendly academics really are.

However, using this to profit from geopolitical outcomes is harder than it looks. The problem is that there are not one, but two difficult questions you need to answer, and you have to get them both right. I'd argue that the odds of doing so consistently are low. Two recent examples demonstrate why.

I. IS THIS A GOOD BET?

First, you have to figure out whether or not you are being offered a good opportunity. To answer that, you need to know: what does the market think, and is my view sufficiently different to make it worth betting against? In the case of buying a cheap stock, this is not especially hard to answer: 'the market is putting "x" price on the stock, I think it's worth at least "y", and even in a worst-case scenario, it's still higher than "x", so it looks a good bet to me.'

But with politics it's trickier. How do you know what's priced into the market and what isn't? Sometimes it's easier than others. The British referendum on leaving the European Union in June 2016 is a good example. Opinion polls consistently showed that the vote was tight – 'Remain' was likely to clinch it, but it was never going to be a clear landslide. However, because most investors and the vast majority of press commentators couldn't conceive of a world where 'Leave' actually won, markets moved very little in the run-up to the vote. The only real tension was in the sterling exchange rate, and even then, on the day before the vote, it was little changed compared to where it had been when the referendum was first called.

So a perceptive contrarian could have identified an opportunity there. The market was certainly too complacent about a Remain victory. As a result, placing a bet on Leave made sense – if Remain won, there was little downside (the market was already pricing that in), and if Leave won there was potentially significant upside (as the market would be shocked and scramble to re-evaluate). As it turned out, the UK did vote to leave the EU.

But these sorts of cut-and-dried political questions and outcomes are rare. Most geopolitical issues are not simple binary outcomes, linked to a specific date, so it's much harder to work out what might be priced in and what isn't. And even when they are, there's a second question you have to get right.

2. IF IT IS A GOOD BET, THEN HOW DO I IMPLEMENT IT?

It's fair to say that betting on a fall in the pound as a result of leaving the EU was an obvious choice. The pound had wobbled any time opinion polls hinted at a Leave victory and rallied when it looked less likely, and it was also the logical response. So a perceptive sceptical investor could have taken a low-risk punt on the pound and made money from the Brexit outcome.

However, it's not always that straightforward. Let's go to another election shocker – Donald Trump's victory in the US presidential elections in November of the same year. As with Brexit, markets, opinion polls and pundits were very confident that there would be no surprises. Hillary Clinton would win – how could she fail against someone like Trump? So the market was – in theory – offering good odds for anyone who wanted to take the opposite side of that bet.

Implementation, however, was a much trickier task. The news was momentarily very bad for stocks, as predicted by countless pundits, and gold shot up too (it tends to do that when instability threatens). Yet by the time the market actually opened that day, it had rebounded to its original level, and then continued higher. So even if you had correctly bet against the political consensus, you may well have struggled to make any money out of it. (The 'correct' bet was to sell the Mexican peso versus the dollar – not quite as obvious a play as the short sterling Brexit trade.)

The point is, be very wary of trying to make money from anything that depends on you both predicting an outcome correctly, and then correctly figuring out the market's reaction. Profiting from forecasting is hard, even if you can become a superforecaster.

Find situations where you don't have to predict the future

A better way to make money from geopolitics is to use market overreactions to invest in assets you already like at cheaper prices than you otherwise could. For example, rather than taking a short-term bet on the pound collapsing after the Brexit vote, you would have been better off looking for opportunities among domestically focused stocks – such as house builders or retailers – which sold off hard in the immediate aftermath of the vote.

Here's an example from the peak of the eurozone crisis in 2012. Greece (and more worryingly, Italy) were viewed as at risk of leaving the single currency in order to escape crippling debt burdens. People thought that the euro was going to break up and that the banking system would go bust. In the end, of course, the European Central Bank (ECB) stepped in to print plenty of money, while citizens in Greece – despite their frustrations – feared the consequences of leaving the euro more than they feared the ongoing pain of staying.

Now, you could have taken an educated punt on the ECB stepping in. That's what every other central bank had done, after all. But let's say that instead you decided to assume the worst – that Greece would crash out of the eurozone and that Italy would be next. When you stepped outside the panic of the moment, you had to accept that – whatever happened to the currency – the underlying assets would still exist. They might be denominated in lire, but they'd certainly still have value. So was that in the price? Well, by this point in mid-2012, Italian stocks were as cheap if not cheaper than they'd been in 2008 (as we noted in the previous chapter, the cyclically-adjusted P/E ratio was at lows only seen on a handful of past occasions) – a point at which the world was worried that the entire financial system was going to come crashing down. If the risk of falling out of the euro wasn't in the price, it was certainly very close to it.

In other words, you didn't have to be able to predict the future to spot a good opportunity. Instead you just needed to find a situation where the downside was pretty much already in the price. That's the real key to sceptical investing – not rolling the dice on your ability to out-forecast the dreaded 'experts'.

CHAPTER

13

Buying Companies for Less Than They're Worth

S O FAR WE'VE been looking at how to approach making money from markets as a whole. What about individual stocks? Value investing is probably the purest form of contrarian investing out there. The efficient market hypothesis argues that the market price of an asset is always right. By contrast, value investors argue that the true value of an asset can be very different from the price that the market puts on it. The value investor makes money by understanding the true value of the asset, then buying or selling when an emotionally driven market offers the opportunity to do so at an advantageous price. As one of the best known and most successful value investors, Seth Klarman, puts it: "Value investing is at its core the marriage of a contrarian streak and a calculator."

I can't teach you how to be a value investor in a single chapter – there are many books you can read on that topic (I have listed several in the bibliography). And each value investor has their own preferred approach – which is partly why, as with many aspects of finance, there are so many debates over what constitutes 'true' value investing.

There are, however, two key concepts that are fundamental to value investing. And these are, I think, also key to understanding some misconceptions about value investing.

What is value investing?

Value investing involves two core concepts: **intrinsic value**, and **margin of safety**. The intrinsic value is what you – the value investor – believe an asset is truly worth. The margin of safety is the gap between its intrinsic value and the price you would feel comfortable buying it at (in order to give you sufficient upside, and also to limit the downside if you are wrong).

So boiling it down (and introducing the one and only equation in this book), a value stock can be considered to be one where:

Current market price < (intrinsic value - percentage margin of safety required)

So if you think that the intrinsic value of a stock is £1, and you require a margin of safety of 30%, then you wouldn't buy until the market offered it to you at 70p or below.

This simple definition immediately flags up a couple of points about value investing. Firstly, both of these measures are highly subjective. The calculation of intrinsic value can be done in lots of different ways. And the margin of safety required will vary from situation to situation.

Secondly, value stocks are traditionally thought of as 'bargain basement' stocks. But this definition makes clear that a stock doesn't necessarily have to be 'cheap' based on simple ratio analysis, or even relative to the rest of the market, in order to be a bargain. A stock could look quite expensive on some measures, but still represent good value, assuming that it is trading sufficiently below its estimated intrinsic value. Equally, a stock can be cheap without being a value stock – it might be cheap for a reason, which is also known as a 'value trap'.

The evolution of value investing – from cigar butts to quality at low prices

Purists may not like this characterisation of value investing. But it reflects the evolution of value investing over the years. Benjamin Graham, Warren Buffett's mentor, is generally accepted as the father of value investing (his books, *Security Analysis* – written with David Dodd – and *The Intelligent Investor*, form the bedrock of the value canon). Graham is often associated with buying distressed stocks that are trading at rock-bottom levels. To a great extent, this was the result of Graham investing during the Depression era, when these sorts of opportunities abounded. In 1932 he wrote a three-part series for *Forbes* magazine, in which he pointed out that almost a third of companies trading on the New York Stock Exchange were trading for less than the value of the cash (or easily liquidated assets) on their balance sheets. In other words, the pavements were scattered with $5 bills and investors were so terrified they were ignoring them.

Graham was also an early proponent of index investing for investors who didn't have the time to dig for bargains, and suggested other techniques in line with an investor's level of experience. But regardless, it's the approach that we might call 'deep value' that he's best known for. And his most famous disciple

– Buffett – at first used similar techniques, or what he called "cigar butt" investing. Here's Buffett, writing in 1989:

> "If you buy a stock at a sufficiently low price, there will usually be some hiccup in the fortunes of the business that gives you a chance to unload at a decent profit, even though the long-term performance of the business may be terrible. I call this the 'cigar butt' approach to investing. A cigar butt found on the street that has only one puff left in it may not offer much of a smoke, but the 'bargain purchase' will make that puff all profit."

But what Buffett realised was that this is a high-risk approach to value investing. For a start, bad businesses tend to have bad luck – they might look cheap today, but another problem is likely just around the corner. "Never is there just one cockroach in the kitchen," as Buffett puts it. Also, you have to be alert to 'flip' them quickly when you get the opportunity to take a profit. Otherwise your money is locked up in a dud business. Again, quoting Buffett: "Time is the friend of the wonderful business, the enemy of the mediocre."

So with the help and persuasion of his business partner Charlie Munger (and the ideas of Philip Fisher, author of another canonical investment book, *Common Stocks and Uncommon Profits*), Buffett moved on to a different model. Rather than trawl through the bargain bin looking for businesses that were worth more dead than alive, Buffett began looking for excellent businesses being sold at a discount to their intrinsic value. As he put it, "It's far better to buy a wonderful company at a fair price than a fair company at a wonderful price."

Some people describe this strategy as 'growth at a reasonable price'. But really it's just value investing given a rebrand (although it's also often abused as a great intellectual fig leaf for fund managers to justify their decisions to buy companies that are already popular).

You can see why buying quality assets at cheap prices might be more appealing than buying poor assets at bargain prices. There are fewer decisions involved – one is a 'buy-and-hold' strategy, whereas the other is a 'buy-to-flip' strategy. The trouble with cigar butts is that you always need to be finding more of them, and there aren't many around. Whereas if you can buy a decent company cheap and then see your return compound up over and over again, then frankly it's less work. There are also fewer risks involved in buying high-quality companies. The big risk with cigar butts is that the market is right. Cheap stocks sometimes just keep getting cheaper, all the way down to zero.

John Maynard Keynes went through a similar intellectual journey to Buffett, when he moved from being a speculator to a value investor (see chapter 9 for more). "As time goes on," he wrote, "I get more and more convinced that the right method in investment is to put fairly large sums into enterprises which one thinks one knows something about and in the management of which one thoroughly believes."

The logic of value investing is hard to resist. And it's inherently contrarian. Why would an asset be trading for a lot less than its intrinsic value in a generally efficient market? Because the crowd has taken against it for irrational, behavioural reasons. Buy while it's out of favour, and you'll do well. The obvious question is: how do you calculate intrinsic value?

How do you calculate intrinsic value?

There are many different approaches to finding value investments, and to have any hope of doing it well, you'll need to have an understanding of how to read a company's accounts, which is beyond the scope of this book (although there are several recommendations in the bibliography for further reading). But to give an idea of the sort of effort that is involved, I want to outline some of the broad principles involved (which will also come in handy if you want to narrow down your hunt for a decent value fund manager to do the hard work on your behalf).

I. LEARN TO IGNORE THE MARKET'S OPINION

This is where the traditional idea of contrarianism and the value investor intersect most closely. The price the market puts on any asset is nothing more than an opinion. You should ignore that opinion. Make up your own mind, and that leaves you ready to act when the market's opinion diverges sufficiently from your own in an advantageous manner. How can you cultivate this mindset?

You are buying a company – not a financial instrument or a gambling chip

Value investors (even the cigar butt variety) approach investing with the mentality of an owner. They don't invest, hoping to be able to sell the shares to someone else, purely because they keep going up. They invest on the basis that they understand the company, and that it is worth more than the current market price. As Buffett puts it, value investors look for "discrepancies between the value of a business and the price of small pieces of that business in the market."

This mentality is useful because it helps you to understand that the value of a company and the price the market puts on that company are two different things. Here are a couple of Buffett sayings that you've almost certainly heard.

> "Price is what you pay. Value is what you get." – *2008 Berkshire Hathaway Letter*

> "To refer to a personal taste of mine, I'm going to buy hamburgers the rest of my life. When hamburgers go down in price, we sing the 'Hallelujah Chorus' in the Buffett household. When hamburgers go up in price, we weep. For most people, it's the same with everything in life they will be buying – except stocks. When stocks go down and you can get more for your money, people don't like them anymore." – 10 December 2001, *Fortune* (with Carol Loomis)

Partly because you've heard them so often and partly because they're couched in that cosy, *Little House on the Prairie*-style cadence that jars outside America, Buffett's comments often sound trite or obvious. But this is actually an extremely profound insight, one worth emphasising.

In the absence of other information, we instinctively look to prices as a guide. It's one technique with which salespeople exploit us (by 'anchoring' our minds to an artificial, higher price, and then offering us a lower one which seems a relative bargain but is in fact nothing of the sort). Yet what Buffett is saying here is that, beyond telling you what an asset can be bought or sold for, price has no informational content for a value investor. The price tag on the asset should not in any way, shape or form influence the price that you are willing to pay for it. This is a valuable lesson and one that aspiring value investors should strive to internalise.

To be clear, this is not the only way to invest. For dedicated technical investors (those who trade based on chart patterns), price is everything – the fundamentals are of no consequence. This is also a valid approach to markets and it works for some people. But if you want to take a value investing approach, your attitude to price should be straightforward. You work out whether a particular company is a business you'd want to own, what price you'd be willing to pay for it, and then you wait for the market to offer it to you at that price. And if it doesn't, then you don't bite.

Understand that risk is about losing money – ups and downs don't matter

One modern-day value investor along these lines is Gary Channon. Since inception in 1998, Channon's Phoenix UK fund has returned nearly 10% a year compared to 5.4% for the FTSE 100 (as of 2018).[5] And of the 88 investments the fund has 'completed', 78% by number were profitable and 88% by value were. In other words, he has a good hit rate in terms of picking the right companies to buy and buying them at a price that later proves to be profitable.

Once a stock has reached the 'right' price for Channon, he buys. As he explains on his fund's website, he has on occasion

5   www.aurorainvestmenttrust.com/cms/assets/163/
az2kmnokquvurfuennzhl5vt/Aurora%20Primer%20January%20
2018.pdf

seen stocks go on to fall by 50% or more from where he first bought them, yet still gone on to make a handsome profit for the fund. How does he do it? Because he has the right approach to risk. "We regard risk as permanent loss of capital," says Channon. That sounds like common sense, but in fact, analysts tend to go on about volatility – a measure of how dramatically an asset's price tends to swing around, relative to the wider market (you can view it as being the bumpiness of the rollercoaster ride you can expect if you invest). "We don't consider volatility to be a risk," says Channon. "If we get our assessment of companies right, then we have nothing to fear from volatility."

2. UNDERSTAND THE BUSINESS INSIDE OUT

If you invest in a bond, you can work out exactly what it should pay you in the future (in nominal terms, i.e. ignoring inflation). As the owner of a bond, you can expect to get the face value of the bond back at maturity, along with whatever interest payments are due between times. So you know how much cash it should generate for you. You can then work out whether you think that this cash flow is worth paying up for today, taking into account the risk that the borrower might not repay you, and whether you could get a better return elsewhere.

Valuing companies involves a similar process. As the owner of the company you are entitled to a share of future profits in the form of dividends (or more controversially, share buybacks). Whatever price you are willing to pay today has to derive from your expectations as to what those future profits will be. But unlike with a bond, you can't put an exact figure on that at the outset. So how can we come to an estimate for intrinsic value?

WHAT ANALYSING COMPANIES BOILS DOWN TO

Ultimately, to have any idea of what a business is worth, you need to answer three questions.

A) How does the business make money?

This often seems like a simple question to answer. But even in businesses that are apparently relatively straightforward, it isn't always. Take the magazine and newspaper publishing business. If you see publishing as primarily a business that makes money by sourcing eyeballs and delivering them to advertisers, then the product is the audience, and the customer is the advertising agency. If you see publishing as primarily a business that makes money by sourcing information and delivering it to readers, then the product is the information, and the customer is the reader. Either model can be made to work and most publishers are a mixture of both. But the challenges involved in each are very different and the key metrics required to measure success are going to be different.

This is where your 'circle of competence' – another concept popularised by Buffett and Munger – comes into play. Your circle of competence – in this context – represents types of businesses that you are familiar with, and understand better than most people. As Buffett put it in his 1996 letter to shareholders, "What an investor needs is the ability to correctly evaluate selected businesses. Note that word 'selected': You don't have to be an expert on every company, or even many. You only have to be able to evaluate companies within your circle of competence." The key, as Buffett puts it, is to understand the difference between what you know, and what you merely think you know. "The size of that circle is not very important; knowing its boundaries, however, is vital." Investors typically come unstuck when they think they know something that then turns out to be false.

This is where beginner investors often get confused. They may have heard Peter Lynch (the extraordinarily successful Fidelity fund manager, and author of *One Up on Wall Street*) talk about buying "what you know". Lynch is not talking about investing in M&S because you like prawn sandwiches and reasonably durable underwear. But if you happen to work for an underwear manufacturer or a sandwich shop that supplies M&S, or you work in logistics and have a deeper understanding of supply chain issues, then that might give you an edge in figuring out what the intrinsic value of M&S should be, for example.

Nor does it mean that you should invest directly in your employer because you understand them better than any other company. For a start, that's way too much concentration risk (you don't want to have both your savings and your income being dependent on the health of a single company), and, secondly, there's a real danger of falling outside the boundaries of your circle of competence – you probably think you know more than you really do about the company that employs you.

Also, you need to have some sector diversification, because you don't want to have all of your eggs in one industry basket. So ideally, you want your circle of competence to cover a number of areas – which is not as hard as it might look, given the range of interests and career experience each of us builds over time. This doesn't mean that you need to be an expert in the first instance, but you do need to develop your knowledge. And it's easier to start from something that you are already familiar with and interested in. For example, I freely admit that I have a poor grasp of tech stocks generally. I quite enjoy gadgets, and I'll certainly get a buzz from buying a new phone or laptop – but I have no sense of what makes one product successful relative to the rest of the market, or what might be the next big thing. So while I might be happy to buy a tech-focused fund if I felt that the tech sector in general was out of favour with the market, I'd avoid investing in individual tech stocks. But talk to me about publishing, or subprime lending (it's a long story), and it's a different matter.

B) Is it any good at it?

Classic value investing involves looking at measures such as price-to-book to see if a company is trading for less than the theoretical value of the assets on its balance sheet. But with this approach, we're trying to see if a company is good at what it does, rather than if it is cheap. And while there are many measures you can look at – and each sector will have its own key metrics, which is where your circle of competence comes in – one useful measure is to look at 'return on capital employed' (ROCE). ROCE looks at a company's trading profit as a percentage of the money invested in the business. In other words, it shows how good a company is at turning money that's been invested in it, into profits. ROCE can help to separate quality companies with sustainable growth from those that are dependent on factors such as acquisitions or financial engineering to flatter earnings and sales figures. As my former colleague and experienced analyst Phil Oakley often points out, ROCE is almost like an interest rate on a savings account – it shows you how hard your money is working, and it also compounds over time, which is crucial to generating market-beating returns in the long run.

You should compare ROCE against the sector average, and the wider market as a whole. But more importantly, you should compare it across time. Look at the company's history – you want to see a consistent or growing ROCE over time, so that the compounding effect gets to work for you. Channon looks for at least 15%. "Most of the money generated by a business is reinvested. If we want excellent returns, then that money needs to be reinvested at high rates. An enduring high rate of return is another sign of a great business."

C) Can it keep it up?

The problem with being a profitable business is that everyone ends up wanting a piece of the action. This is at the heart of how free market capitalism works. Entrepreneurs spot an opportunity to make money. One of them cracks it, and makes a lot of money. Other entrepreneurs notice that someone else has discovered a honey pot, and they all swarm over. Eventually, only the most efficient operators survive. As a result, they make just enough profit, while consumers and the wider economy benefit from scarce resources being used efficiently.

This is – perhaps counter-intuitively, as the ongoing appeal of centralised systems demonstrates – a good way to manage and distribute resources. But it's a pretty brutal environment in which to make a living. So if you're a shareholder, you want the company to be able to maintain its lead on the competition for as long as possible. As Buffett put it in 2011: "The single most important decision in evaluating a business is pricing power. If you've got the power to raise prices without losing business to a competitor, you've got a very good business. And if you have to have a prayer session before raising the price 10%, then you've got a terrible business."

The advantages that make pricing power possible are collectively known as an 'economic moat'. Given that profit margins are generally competed away over time, a consistently high ROCE and stable margins are good quantitative signals that a company has a decent moat. In terms of qualitative judgements, you need to understand what that moat consists of, and whether or not it is sustainable. For example, a company may have a powerful brand (such as Coca-Cola or Apple). Or it might own a lot of patents. Or it might be protected from competition by a wall of regulation (tobacco companies being the most obvious example). Equally, a company's dominance might be threatened with political intervention if it becomes too obviously powerful within its niche – social media giant Facebook is one example. Put simply, what is the company's competitive advantage, and will it last?

The most important characteristic of management – integrity

What role does management play in all this? Different fund managers have different views. Some like to talk to management regularly. Others prefer to avoid meeting them at all. Buffett notes that if a company has a big enough moat, it doesn't need to have a great manager in order to thrive. Other than small companies, the average private investor is unlikely to secure a sit-down meeting with a chief executive. And even if you could, it might not be a great idea – an individual's charisma (or lack of it) can easily influence your decisions rather than adding anything useful to your evaluation of a company.

Instead, as Channon puts it, when it comes to management, "most importantly we look at their integrity or for signs of its absence." One of the biggest enemies of the value investor is outright fraud, or borderline fraud, which is often due more to incompetence, negligence and backside-covering, rather than deliberate bad behaviour. You have a situation where the books say the company is cheap, but the books, unfortunately, are cooked (legally or illegally – both are possible).

So how can you guard against this? No approach is foolproof – even the sharpest investors get taken in (in the 1980s, Sir John Templeton was a big holder of FTSE 100 conglomerate Polly Peck, for example, which collapsed in 1990 following an investigation by the Serious Fraud Office). But as we noted in chapter 8, red flags to watch for include celebrity CEOs (they get to be celebrities by having big egos, and people with big egos tend to overreach themselves); badly designed incentive schemes; and managers who have no skin in the game. A decent track record helps too – if someone has dealt honestly in their career to date, they are unlikely to change now. But in reality, your best defence against bad or fraudulent management is to have a good understanding of the business yourself. That means you can then spot when management is either trying to pull the wool over your eyes, or perhaps even spot impending problems (perhaps stemming from lack of investment) before management does.

3. ALWAYS REMEMBER THAT PATIENCE IS YOUR GREATEST WEAPON

A sceptical, value-driven approach is all about taking advantage of market turmoil and the instinctive, gut-driven reactions of others in order to pick up assets while they are temporarily trading at good prices. That takes patience. How do you cultivate this trait?

The best time to do your research is now – build a watchlist

Channon and his team demand a hefty margin of safety – they aim to pay no more than half of a business's intrinsic value. So that means a lot of sitting around. "We wait for the opportunity to invest at attractive prices. This can take years and may never happen." However, "occasionally the market overreacts to short-term negative developments." This is one reason why busts can be so profitable for sceptical investors – indiscriminate selling is a great opportunity to pick up decent companies at low prices. "We view market turmoil as an opportunity."

But there's only one way to be ready to take advantage of such an opportunity – you need to do the work in advance. The best time to do this research is right now. You don't want to be left scrabbling around in the middle of a crisis, trying to figure out whether or not a given company is now a bargain or is on the verge of bankruptcy. Without a solid, pre-existing understanding of a company, you are more likely than not to make a mistake. So start hunting down good companies and working out their intrinsic value now.

Be very wary of leverage

The power that patience gives you is the ability to hang on when other investors are acting impulsively in reaction to the price, rather than the value, of an asset. Leverage is like kryptonite to this contrarian superpower. If you borrow money to buy an asset, there is always the risk that the lender calls in the loan (known as a 'margin call') at precisely the worst moment. If you use leverage, you are transforming volatility risk – a risk that sceptical investors can ignore to their advantage – into a genuine risk, one that can cause the permanent loss of capital. That's why so many people lose so much money spread betting – even when their long-term view is correct, the short term involves too much volatility to be capable of remaining in a position.

Leverage is not solely a function of your own borrowing as an investor. In general, the more leverage a company uses (the more 'highly geared' it is), the riskier it is. This doesn't mean that you should avoid all companies and sectors that use debt. But a value investor must have a particularly tight focus on the state of the balance sheet, the cash flow statement, and solvency risks. Debt, if improperly managed, can destroy an otherwise successful business overnight.

Don't be afraid to focus

It may sound as though true value opportunities are few and far between, and that's true. But on the flipside, you don't need to find all that many of them. While it's sensible to diversify between sectors, full-on value investors rarely own a huge number of individual stocks. You only have time to monitor a limited number of stocks, and most Buffett-style managers aim for 10 to

25 (with 25 really being a maximum). Also, bear in mind that, as a private investor, this is likely only part of your portfolio – you can (and should) achieve diversification by having another chunk of your overall wealth invested in an index fund (more on which in a moment).

Wow. This sounds like hard work – can we automate it?

You probably now understand why Buffett says that about 80% of his working day is taken up with "reading and thinking". Finding good companies at good prices is hard, time-consuming work, and there are many more aspects to spotting quality companies than I can go into here (if you're planning to go down this route, among other things, I'd recommend reading Oakley's book, *How to Pick Quality Shares*). I'd like to be able to say that there's some magic number or a secret to all of this – but if there was, then everyone would be doing it, and it wouldn't work anymore.

So what's the alternative? These days, there are many exchange-traded funds (ETFs) that focus on value, as it is one of several strategies (or 'factors') that historic data analysis suggests leads to consistent outperformance of the wider market. In other words, if you buy stocks that look cheap – even on a mechanical, ratio-based basis – then you should win over the long run. This argument makes sense, and over time value *does* tend to win out. According to Bank of America Merrill Lynch, between 1926 and 2016, value stocks returned 17% a year on average, compared to just 12.6% for growth, and value beat growth in roughly three years out of five.

If you want to pursue more traditional value investing, then this is a straightforward way to do it in a diversified manner, which will help you to offset the inevitable risk that you end up with a portfolio full of value traps. The problem with traditional value ratios is that a low price-to-earnings (P/E) ratio can indicate either that the share price is too low – or that earnings are about to fall off a cliff; a low price-to-book ratio can indicate that the price is too low – or that the balance sheet is overstated; and a high dividend yield can indicate that a price is too low – or that the dividend is about to be slashed. Buying a fund gives you the diversification you need if you feel unable to do the necessary legwork to make buying individual 'deep value' stocks a viable proposition.

However, there are a few points I'd make. One is that you have to be prepared for long periods in which value underperforms both the wider market and its great rival, growth investing. For example, in the decade following the financial crisis, growth trounced value, partly because low interest rates and low growth expectations made investors willing to pay a significant premium for the few companies with apparently stellar growth prospects. Typically, you can tell that one of these periods is coming to an end when headlines appear asking plaintively, "Is value investing dead?" or " Is Warren Buffett past it?"

Secondly, as with anything else you buy, you have to make sure that you understand what's actually in the fund. For a start, how does it define 'value', and what universe of stocks can it draw from? Different ETFs use different measures to screen for value. Also, the value factor – as with many factors – is arguably more pronounced among small-cap stocks (depending on which studies you believe) so it's worth looking for value ETFs with as broad a scope as possible.

Finally, remember that whenever you buy an ETF, you will always be getting relative value, as opposed to absolute value. In other words, if stocks in general are expensive, then the value options might be cheap compared to other stocks, but not especially cheap – and perhaps even expensive – relative to history. If this is the case, you might be better off looking for an entirely different, cheaper global market to invest in, as discussed in Chapter 11.

Overall, relying on an ETF to give you performance is not going to be as good as picking decent-quality value stocks at the right time, nor from finding an active manager who can do the same. But, of course, buying an ETF is a lot easier than finding managers who can pull this off, or doing it yourself. Perhaps the lesson is, as hedge fund manager and 'factor' expert Clifford Asness and his colleagues Andrea Frazzini, Ronen Israel and Tobias Moskowitz put it in a 2015 research paper, to "consider both".[6]

6   www.valuewalk.com/2015/04/aqr-white-paper-fact-fiction-and-value-investing

CHAPTER

14

Turnaround Situations, Falling Knives & Profit Warnings

"THE US GOVERNMENT is starting a propaganda campaign to make BP public enemy number one. They've had Saddam Hussein and they've had Osama and now it's BP. And you don't want to make an investment where you are fighting the US government."

It was the middle of June 2010. I was hosting a roundtable discussion at the *MoneyWeek* offices with a group of fund managers to get their views on the best opportunities in the market. I'd just asked them for their views on UK oil giant, BP. Suffice to say, it was a controversial topic.

Just two months earlier, an explosion on the Deepwater Horizon, a BP-operated drilling rig in the Gulf of Mexico, had killed 11 crewmen and left oil gushing into the sea. It was one of the biggest stories to hit the business pages since the 2008 financial crisis, and emotions were running high. Men had lost their lives. The oil spill threatened livelihoods all across the Louisiana coast. The American public was understandably appalled, and the sense that a foreign company was responsible for the carnage added an undercurrent of hostility that the British press was very happy to play up, particularly given that President Barack Obama was perceived to have a somewhat cool attitude towards Britain.

To make matters worse, BP had badly mishandled its response. The company had entirely failed to get ahead of the story. It downplayed the scale of the problem in the early stages, and then continued to make a series of tone-deaf, insensitive gaffes, which would eventually led to CEO Tony Hayward stepping down later that year. It was, in every sense, a disaster.

However, BP's share price had been hammered, collapsing from a high of above £6.40, just before the spill, to around £3.50. And the tone of the commentary was growing hyperbolic. The idea that the US government would actually go out of its way to put BP out of business – bearing in mind that this multinational company employed a significant number of American citizens – seemed unlikely. So when this manager sat back and told me that under no circumstances would he buy it, citing BP in the same breath as the US military's biggest bête noire, I thought: 'Hmm, maybe it's time to buy BP.'

At the end of that month – just two weeks after the meeting – the BP share price hit rock bottom, falling to just under £3 at its lowest point before it rebounded. The Deepwater disaster was by no means over – the potential legal liabilities continued to hang over BP for years – but the market had realised that the company, while facing significant costs and reputational damage, wasn't going to go bankrupt. Within eight months the price had risen back to nearly £5 a share – a very healthy gain in a very short period of time for anyone who bought at or near the bottom.

Why you shouldn't rush to catch falling knives

These sorts of stories are catnip for investors. They're the sorts of high-profile contrarian trades that you can brag about afterwards if you get them right. And this is one reason that I've singled them out for special treatment. Because this is precisely the sort of investment where an aspiring sceptical investor can really come a cropper.

Stocks which tumble after being hit by profit warnings or bad news that comes out of the blue, are often described in the City as 'falling knives'. That's because it can really hurt if you try to catch them on the way down. Don't get me wrong – some people are very good at catching them. And we'll look at some indicators that might indicate that a company's woes are fully priced in further on in this chapter.

But if you pride yourself on being a sceptical investor, then you should be extra sceptical of any company whose share price has just slid off the edge of a cliff. You might be thinking: 'What's the point of being a contrarian if you don't buy when everyone else is selling?' To which my response would be: 'What's the point of being a contrarian if you just lose money all day hand over fist because you can't resist taking random punts on collapsing stocks on the questionable premise that they'll one day get their mojo back?'

There are lots of ways to be contrarian – buying individual stocks is just a small part of it. For example, getting the asset class or sector you invest in correct is often far more important than your individual holdings – so if you can find a market or a sector that is cheap and neglected (see chapter 10), then that can be a very lucrative and less risky way for a sceptical investor to make money, without taking any individual stock risk.

So I'm going to outline the risks upfront, and only then talk about the sorts of indicators you might want to watch for if you really want to play around with these companies. The key thing to remember is this: be patient. There will always be other opportunities.

I. BUYING AND SELLING PSYCHOLOGY MEANS THAT DOWNTURNS RARELY END QUICKLY

As soon as a company runs into trouble – particularly a big, brand-name, headline-grabbing company – your bargain-hunting instinct will probably kick in, especially if you've had your eye on the stock. Your brain will be screaming: 'Buy! Any minute now, the market is going to bounce.' Stop. Take a deep breath. This is anchoring at work. Your brain can't let go of the top left-hand side of the share price chart. It's struggling to cope with the idea that a share that was worth £1 yesterday is now selling for 60p. This old information – the idea that the share is 'worth' £1 – is now obsolete and misleading. You need time to incorporate the new information about the company into your mental picture of it.

The good news is, on average, you have plenty of time. Research is mixed, but most studies show that, in the first instance, markets under-react to profit warnings. That's because, at the same time as your brain is screaming 'buy', the owners of the stock are wincing and looking at their trading screens from behind their fingers. They don't want to crystallise their losses – taking a loss, even a small one, makes us feel stupid and like we've wasted our time. (From a behavioural point of view, we also ascribe additional value to something we already own, which is known as the 'endowment effect' but is really just an extension of confirmation bias – we value things that we own because they form part of our world view, and we hate being forced to jettison them because that means acknowledging that this aspect of our world view may be wanting.)

In other words, when a profit warning hits, human instinct dictates that sellers on average won't sell aggressively enough, and all too many buyers will be ready to jump in too early. So it's highly unlikely that the immediate, initial fall is going to be sufficient, unless the warning itself has been heavily over-exaggerated, badly communicated, or is reversed (which is also highly unlikely).

The statistics bear this theory out. Paul Scott and the team at Stockopedia looked at 245 profit warnings from small companies between January 2013 and August 2016.[7] They found that, on average, the share price of a company that warns on profits keeps falling, and only puts in a temporary bottom about six months after the initial warning. It then typically reaches a lower bottom within another six months. Similarly, a study by George Bulkley, Richard Harris and Renata Herrerias of the department of economics at Exeter University, which looked at 455 companies issuing profit warnings between 1997 and 1999, found that prices tended to take at least six months, if not longer, to hit rock bottom.[8]

7   assets.stockopedia.com/ebooks/profit-warnings/published/profit-warnings.pdf
8   pdfs.semanticscholar.org/8da0/6dda8c01fb1fb2f3a428b3435532b51378d2.pdf?_ga=2.136366260.526002484.1519919959-1439590237.1519919959

2. WHY DO YOU CARE ABOUT THIS STOCK ANYWAY?

There is nothing wrong with seeing a profit warning as the beginning of a potential buying opportunity. However, if the company isn't already on your watchlist, be extra wary. It indicates that the company has never previously cropped up on your radar as a decent prospect, which suggests that it is outside your circle of competence. Instead, you've been drawn to it for the wrong reason – you're focusing on the falling price, rather than on finding a good business. The good news is that – as the statistics above suggest – you typically have about a year between the profit warning hitting and the stock starting on the road to recovery (assuming it does). That gives you plenty of time to conduct proper due diligence, along the lines of the framework we outlined in chapter 13, before you think about investing. Once again – when it comes to successful sceptical investing, patience pays off.

3. CAN THIS BE FIXED? OR IS IT THE BEGINNING OF SOMETHING MUCH WORSE?

An old City saying has it that profit warnings come in threes. Like many City sayings, this isn't literally true, but it's fair to say that the first profit warning is very rarely the end of the story. A profit warning is, by its very nature, unexpected – if it was expected, the company wouldn't have to issue it. As a result, it's always difficult to quantify the damage, and even if the company attempts to do so, it's hard to rely on its figures. After all, if its previous forecasts were wrong, how can we be sure that the new ones are any more accurate? Remember – as sceptical investors, we're looking to buy a decent company for the long run. The profit warning might give us the opportunity to do that. But we also need to be very aware of the downside. There are always other opportunities, and it's far better to let a 50/50 decision that ends up turning out well go by you, rather than taking a punt on a fallen angel that ends up eviscerating your portfolio.

As the investment managers at fund group AKO note in their book *Quality Investing*, profit warnings need to be taken very seriously. "A material profit warning, even from a company in a relatively stable industry, can indicate that serious internal problems are brewing, suggesting a need to fully reevaluate the investment thesis ... overall deterioration generally begins with small things not going according to plan: growth not materialising, unexplained pressure on margins, more discussion of competitive pressures, or gradual increases in capital expenditure. Each disappointment is small in isolation; management provides a good explanation for each and dismisses them as non-recurring. But a string of setbacks often signals a larger set of problems."

Separating the recovery plays from the walking wounded

The point of all these caveats is this: if you're going to run the slide rule over a troubled company, make sure you approach it with even more caution than usual. You might pick up a stock that's ripe for recovery. On the other hand, you might end up with a long-term value trap – a stock that's stuck in decline –

or, worse still, a stock that's imminently on its way to zero (like outsourcing group Carillion, for example). Remember: a stock that has fallen by 90%, started out as a stock that had fallen by 80% – and then lost another 50% of its value. So what should you be looking out for to distinguish between temporary setbacks and the beginning of the end?

'One-off' incidents: finding the worst-case scenario

Any number of disasters can hit a company. Some are easier to categorise than others. For example, horrendous as they are, oil spills are an occupational hazard of investing in oil companies. You could argue that it signals that the company has neglected to invest in safety (which is something you would probably want to look at), but equally, it's not necessarily a sign of a deeper, existential malaise – it doesn't mean that the company's business model is broken or that it is in long-term decline. Similarly, if a highly hyped pharmaceutical product fails at the last clinical trial hurdle – again, it doesn't necessarily signal anything systemic about a big drugs company. It's a piece of bad news, but it should be quantifiable, using scenario planning and comparing with similar incidents. The key here is to gauge the likely cost, and then work out whether the market is underpricing the stock badly enough to give you a sufficient margin of safety as an investor.

Of course, to get an idea of whether the market is pricing in a worst-case scenario you have to have an idea of what the worst-case scenario is. That requires research and a bit of educated guesswork. Oldfield Partners are value investors, who began investing in BP in 2010 pretty much at the low – three months after the spill. As Richard Oldfield explains in the notes to one of the boutique's 2016 investor days, the rationale was as follows: "On the whole, these huge class-action suits result in enormous figures being bandied around, which do not come through. For example with BP, figures being talked about were of $100–120bn." So they used $120bn as their worst-case scenario, and then, using a probability-weighted model (in other words, ascribing odds to each outcome and then averaging them out) came to a loss figure of around $60bn, which in fact, is pretty much what the spill ended up costing BP over the long run. Based on that, they felt there was a sufficient margin of safety built in.[9]

Oldfield did something similar with Volkswagen. The German car maker scandalised the world in 2015 when it turned out to have fiddled results of emissions tests to make its cars look greener than they really were. As Richard Garstang of Oldfield points out: "There was fear, there was panic, and a significant fall in the share price and we started looking at the company and the issues it faced in great detail straight away." Put simply, Garstang and his team worked out what they believed the underlying business – which is home to brands from Audi to Porsche to Skoda – was worth. They assumed the company would lose market share and be subject to more competitive pressure (and thus lower profit margins) as a result of the scandal. There were then various other parts of the company, such as its truck business, financial services arm, and joint ventures in China, that hadn't been touched

9 www.valuewalk.com/wp-content/uploads/2016/06/ Globalinvestordaytranscript14.03.2016.pdf

by the scandal, and which had significant value in themselves. Using conservative assumptions, they reckoned the company – before potential liabilities from the emissions scandal – was worth roughly twice what it was trading for. They then looked at potential recall costs (given the number of cars affected) and spoke to lawyers about potential legal penalties, given historic fines faced by other car manufacturers for recalls. Even with these thrown in, the company was – conservatively – still worth about 40% more than the market value at the time.

As you can see, this process of quantifying the damage takes a lot of work (although, even as a private investor, if you are confident enough to wrap your head around the figures, you should be able to compile your own view using publicly available data in most cases), and also hangs on a number of assumptions. That's why, as Oldfield notes, "we don't want too much of the portfolio in similar situations ... We class these types of investment as being in 'toxic corner', where there is a significant downside risk, but if the downside doesn't materialise the upside is huge."

Does the market hate this stock yet?

Another aspect – once you've worked out a rough fair value for the stock – is to consider sentiment. In the early stages of a profit-warning-driven collapse, a stock is besieged by bargain hunters, desperately trying to time the rally. Most of these investors are badly burned, because as we noted above, even as they are trying to 'buy the dips', injured owners of the stock are aiming to 'sell the rips' – that is, get out with a slightly smaller loss than they feared they'd have to take.

So as the news gets worse and the share price steadily falls, more and more investors end up being hurt by the stock. Eventually, there comes a point of maximum revulsion where investors feel so disillusioned and burned by the scandal-hit stock that they go from hoping to pick up a bargain to being unwilling to buy at any price. Hope turns to disgust, and at that point, it's open season, and the market is highly likely to overestimate rather than underestimate the damage.

For me, what signalled the turning point for BP was the fact that a fund manager could happily compare the company to the world's most wanted terrorist – and do so on record – without worrying that it might sound ridiculous. It was also a good example of the 'inside' versus the 'outside' view in action. The fund manager was looking at the specifics of the case – the inside view – and making his judgement based on the perception of a hostile political administration that had the opportunity to stick it to a foreign company. However, taking the outside view, if you looked at comparable incidents (such as the 1989 *Exxon Valdez* spill) as a benchmark, you could rapidly conclude that whatever else was going to happen to BP, it was highly unlikely to be driven out of business.

The first cockroach is rarely the last – the archetypal profit warning journey

One-off warnings caused by specific, broadly quantifiable incidents are often shocking and headline-grabbing but they are also often relatively quick to resolve. Events unfold rapidly, the scale of the damage becomes clear, and the market can make a judgement one way or another. However, in other cases, the problem is more subtle, and typically more pernicious. In fact, if we were to try to put together an archetypal profit warning 'journey', then I'd say that the milestones would probably look something like this.

I. DENIAL: "IT'S JUST A FLESH WOUND"

At this stage, the company warns that profits aren't going to quite meet expectations. They'll state the case in cagey terms, and they might even try to avoid calling it a profit warning. This is because the management team knows that investors will be surprised and disappointed, and that they're going to wonder why the highly skilled management team in charge of the company wasn't already on top of the issue. So they feel defensive, and inclined to downplay any problems.

Take aerospace engineer Rolls-Royce. In early 2014, the stock was flying high. From a financial-crisis low point of below £3 in late 2008, the share price had risen to more than £12. The company had enjoyed a strong 2013, and while peers in the sector had been hit by cuts to US defence budgets, Rolls-Royce had thus far remained immune.

But then, in February 2014, alongside its full-year results, Rolls issued its first profit warning in a decade, noting that both sales and profit growth for the year ahead would be flat – primarily as the result of the same US defence cuts that had hurt others in its sector. The share price fell by nearly 14% on the day to

£10.45. Chief executive John Rishton was somewhat defensive when asked why Rolls hadn't clarified the situation to analysts earlier: "We always give guidance at this stage, with the full-year results. Whether people are happy, sad or indifferent is for them to think about." And he reassured the market that it was just a temporary issue. "This is a pause, not a change in direction, and growth will resume in 2015." This sort of denial is a classic sign that a company has not confronted its problems, and is heading for a follow-up profit warning.

Another good example came from doorstep lender Provident Financial in 2017. In June, shares in the company fell by nearly 20% when chief executive Peter Crook issued a trading update. A major restructuring of its workforce – replacing self-employed door-to-door agents with full-time staff armed with iPads – had disrupted the debt collection process badly, resulting in a significant rise in uncollected payments, and a drop in new loans written. Nevertheless, Crook noted that "the strategic rationale for the change remains strong and I am confident that it will deliver the substantial benefits previously communicated."

2. REALITY BITES: "OOPS, WE DID IT AGAIN"

Of course, by the time investors get to hear about the problem, things are already bad, and almost certainly worse than anyone is letting on – otherwise management wouldn't announce it at all. So unless it's clear that a solution is already in place, and management has taken things in hand, the situation is only likely to deteriorate further. And that's often what happens. AKO studied profit warnings at nearly 650 European companies from the start of 2004 to the second quarter of 2013 (excluding the crisis years of 2007 and 2008 to avoid skewing the sample). They found that if a warning resulted in an initial share price decline of 10% or more, then subsequent performance was likely to be bad, and about a third of such profit warnings were followed by another, even bigger profit warning, within the year. In other words, the bigger the shock, the harder the fall.

Here's what happened at Rolls-Royce. In October 2014, it warned on profits again – sales would now fall, rather than remain flat, and both sales and profits would be flat or a little lower in 2015. This time the share price fell by 11% on the day, closing at 832p – more than 30% lower than the share price prior to the first warning. The company blamed plunging oil prices and a deteriorating economic backdrop. Rishton was still somewhat defensive – "we can't control what is going on in the external environment" – but clearly the pressure was on.

3. TIME FOR A CHANGE: "IT'S NOT YOU, IT'S – WELL, ACTUALLY IT *IS* YOU"

There may or may not be further specific profit warnings. But typically, after the second profit warning, if not before, the market starts to get edgy and loses faith in top management. So you'll often see changes at the top, and often it's the CEO or the chief financial officer (or both) who end up leaving.

For example, Provident Financial's second profit warning was rather more dramatic than that of Rolls-Royce. In August – just two months after the original warning – the company admitted that debt collection levels had collapsed, and that it would now make a loss for the year. The share price plunged by 66% on the day, the interim dividend was scrapped, and Crook had no choice but to fall on his sword.

Rolls-Royce's journey was slower. In November 2014, a month after its second profit warning. Rolls started cutting jobs and its finance director (who had struggled to communicate the state of the accounts) left. In February 2015, Rolls issued a weak set of results, but they were no worse than the market's lowered expectations, and the share price rallied. By April 2015, when Rishton stepped down as CEO of his own accord, and Warren East – a darling of the tech world – took over, the market had started to believe that Rolls was getting on top of its problems, and the share price was back above £10.

4. RESETTING EXPECTATIONS: "EVERYTHING INCLUDING THE KITCHEN SINK"

A change at the top is often a good sign. Once the original management team is shaken up, the new bosses have a clean slate to take any action necessary. Also, if the new boss is willing to take the job at all, it suggests that there is still hope (that's not always the case but few CEOs are willing to take the helm at a complete basket case). Meanwhile, a dividend cut is often a good sign too – it shows that the company means business. Managements dislike cutting the dividend, because they know that shareholders hate it when the dividend goes. So if they grasp that nettle, it shows that they know how serious things are.

So what tends to happen is that the new CEO kicks the tyres, tuts loudly, and exaggerates just how bad everything is (this is known as 'kitchen sinking'). The share price often falls hard to reflect that – but it's at this point that you know the company is finally close to, or has managed to get ahead of, the problem.

This process may take a bit of time. For example, at Rolls-Royce, in July 2015, on East's second day in the job, he issued yet another profit warning. He had to scrap an ill-advised share buyback scheme (launched under his predecessor), while he got to grips with the poor visibility of revenues and Rolls' incredible sensitivity to changes in the economic backdrop.

But it was November before the real whopper came. The dividend was put under review, profit estimates were slashed, and East effectively said that the entire company needed to overhaul the way that it worked. The share price collapsed by 20% on the day, to a low of just above £5. In all, the share price had more than halved since the start of 2014.

And yet, that climactic profit warning pretty much marked the bottom for the shares. That's partly because they'd fallen so hard and were genuinely cheap by that point. But it's also because East was able to come in, with no prior connection to Rolls-Royce, and no need to defend previous working practices or the existing business model – after all, it wasn't his fault. So he had every reason to hit investors with as much bad news as possible (as a CEO, you want to get the bad news over at the start of your reign, so that by the end you can point to a share price that's higher than when you began, all because of your efforts).

'Kitchen sinking' may be somewhat cynical, but it does seem to work. AKO found that companies with recent CEO changes tend to profit warn "a bit more frequently" than those with no change – but those that do warn after chief executive changes tend to go on to beat the index.

The red flags that scream 'do not touch'

So we can see how one-off warnings can potentially lead to buying opportunities, and even 'cockroach' warnings can culminate in a good buying opportunity. But what red flags might make you avoid a stock altogether?

- **Heavily shorted stocks:** if short sellers target the company you are investing in or are thinking of investing in, you should pay attention. Revisit your thesis for investing with some urgency, and make sure that you really understand what's going on. Short sellers don't always get it right, but the high levels of risk involved mean that they have a strong incentive to do their research. Being long and wrong is a slow road to the poor house – the opportunity cost can be high and if you don't act to cut your losers quickly, you can erode away your wealth in a painful manner. But being short and wrong is a motorway to misery. If you are betting on a share price falling, your losses are technically unlimited – a share price can only go to zero, but there is no ceiling on its price. It also costs money to hold a short position for an extended period of time. So short sellers need to have higher conviction than the average long – they not only have to get the direction right, but they also have to consider the timing much more carefully.

This isn't just theoretical – a study by Ferhat Akbas, Ekkehart Boehmer, Bilal Erturk, and Sorin Sorescu from 2008 classified short sellers as "highly informed traders", and found that "high levels of short interest predict negative abnormal returns."[10] In other words, there's rarely smoke without a fire. So if you own a stock that's widely shorted, make sure that you understand both what the short sellers' rationale is, and why you believe that it is wrong. In fact, I would write that down in your investment journal – 'why the short sellers are wrong on this company'. Also, be wary if company management blames short sellers for their woes. That's a very good sign that they're covering up for something else. The UK regulator, the Financial Conduct Authority, publishes a spreadsheet (updated daily) of short positions in the London market, which several websites have compiled into a more user-friendly format – it's worth monitoring.

- **Beware complicated accounting or changes to accounting standards over time:** If you can't understand where the money is coming from in a company, or it makes changes to its accounting methodology for reasons that it can't explain or that don't sound reasonable, then give it a wide berth. The key with profit warnings is that you need to see the company tackling the underlying problem, not covering it up. As AKO point out: "Accounting shenanigans manifest in many ways, including premature revenue recognition, inflated gross margins, improperly capitalised expenses, depleting reserves and manipulating cash flows. Many of these areas include some

10 pdfs.semanticscholar. org/0641/8ef437dc7156229532a97d0f8392373eb297.pdf

degree of judgement. However, when these judgements start to move beyond the realms of reasonableness, our experience is that it is usually a mistake to ignore them: such accounting red flags can be powerful indicators that the underlying business is also deteriorating."

- **Beware of debt:** most companies require debt at some point in their existence. Debt can help a company to grow, or to manage its day-to-day operations efficiently. However, few things can destroy a company more rapidly than a debt burden that it can no longer service. Shareholders should be particularly wary of debt, because every single debtor a company owes money to stands in front of shareholders, in terms of having a claim on the company's carcass, should it go bust. There are many ways to analyse a company's balance sheet – too many to go into here (again, I recommend part two of Phil Oakley's *How to Pick Quality Shares* for an in-depth explanation of how to test for both visible and 'hidden' debts) – but if a company warns on profits, and you have any concerns that it is at risk of breaching its banking covenants or being unable to raise money from the market, then steer well clear.

What if a stock I already own turns into a falling knife? Twist or fold – don't stick

So far we've talked about buying companies that have been hit by profit warnings. But what if you already own one? The good news is that the correct way to deal with this is simple. The bad news is that it's not easy. In his short but punchy book, *The Art of Execution*, fund of funds manager Lee Freeman-Shor looked at nearly 2,000 individual investments made by managers at his fund between 2006 and 2013. He uncovered some interesting and sobering statistics. Of 131 investments where the share price had fallen by more than 40% from a manager's original buying point, not a single one recovered sufficiently to make back the initial loss (the companies didn't necessarily go bust – they just didn't make it back to their previous highs). So when you're faced with a disaster scenario, you can't ignore it and hope that it'll go away (or that the share price will recover to a point where you can break even and salvage your pride). Instead, you have just two stark choices: sell and cut your losses right away, or buy more, with the hope of profiting sufficiently from a recovery in the price to still make a profit in the longer run (also known as 'averaging down').

Freeman-Shor notes that either strategy can be successful. The fund managers that he rated as investors came from both categories. But the point was, they didn't dither – they took action. "The only solution to a losing situation is to sell out or significantly increase your stake." Ask yourself one simple question, he says: "If I had a blank piece of paper and were looking to invest today, would

I buy into that stock given what I now know? If your answer to the question … is 'No', or 'maybe, but…' then you should sell."

The real beauty of this strategy is that it forces you to take action. And in most cases, except where you have extraordinary levels of conviction, the answer is almost certainly going to be 'sell' and move on. Indeed, Freeman-Shor recommends setting automated stop-losses — set at somewhere between 20% and 33% from the most recent high — as a good way to keep you honest. This is something you have to decide for yourself – I've heard arguments from some good fund managers that it makes no sense to set stop-losses, but those are usually from confident, high-conviction managers who know their stocks inside out and clearly plan to buy and hold forever unless something drastic changes. I would strive for that level of clarity and conviction, but in its absence it's also worth being realistic about your own limitations.

CHAPTER

15

*Finding a
Contrarian Fund
Manager*

B Y N O W , Y O U ' V E probably realised at least one thing: successful contrarian investing is hard. If you've decided that it's more trouble than it's worth, you might want to get a fund manager to do it for you. But how do you choose a decent one?

Finding a fund manager who can outperform the market on a long-term basis is not easy. A very small number of managers achieve it, but the problem is identifying them in the first place. Indeed, one of the main arguments for passive investing over active investing is the sheer difficulty of finding managers who will do well over time.

That said, there are ways to increase your odds of finding a quality manager. So if you don't feel comfortable or able to put in the necessary time to invest in stocks or other assets on your own behalf, here are some of the traits you need to look for when researching active funds to find a contrarian manager.

1. Look for a defined, transparent strategy and a process that they can explain to you

The first important thing is to find managers who have defined strategies that they can easily articulate to you. Successful investment is tricky but the principles are not hard, so it should be more than possible for a knowledgeable fund manager with any degree of enthusiasm and conviction to explain their process to a reasonably intelligent adult like yourself.

Understanding how the fund is meant to work is critical. David Swensen – who, as manager of the Yale University endowment, has access to the most elaborate investment strategies and costly hedge funds that you can imagine – has this to say about investing in 'quantitative' strategies, which in effect rely on complex algorithms to find patterns in markets worth pursuing.

> "I have never been a big fan of quantitative approaches to investment. And the fundamental reason is that I can't understand what's in the black box. And if I don't know what's in the black box, and there's underperformance, I don't know if the black box is broken or if it's out of favour. And if it's broken, you want to stop. And if it's out of favour, you want to increase your exposure.

> "And so I'm an old-fashioned guy that wants to sit across the table from somebody who's done the analysis and understand why they own the position. And then if it goes against them, I can have another conversation and try and figure out whether the thesis was wrong and we should exit, or whether the thesis is intact and we should increase the position."[11]

This isn't necessarily to say that there's anything wrong with using algorithms. But the point to take from Swensen is that you need to be in a position where you can make a judgement as to whether a manager's strategy makes sense; whether it fits in with your portfolio; and whether they are actually sticking to it with sufficient conviction. 'Style drift' is probably one of the biggest

11 awealthofcommonsense.com/2017/11/swensen

risks you need to watch out for with active funds, because if you think you own one thing, and in fact you own another, it can potentially derail your whole carefully planned asset allocation.

Now, you won't necessarily be able to talk directly to the fund manager before you invest with them. But the best managers make communication a priority. Nick Train of Finsbury Growth & Income has an extremely clear investment strategy: buy companies with durable consumer brands, run a nice, concentrated portfolio, don't trade too often, and ignore macroeconomics entirely in favour of a long-term permabullish outlook. Gary Channon's Phoenix website is full of easy-to-read documentation explaining the company's investment philosophy and process, as well as videos outlining individual case studies (both successful investments and less successful ones). Alasdair McKinnon at the Scottish Investment Trust has a very explicit set of three categories into which he slots each of his stock picks. And of course, Warren Buffett – who in reality runs an exceptionally complicated group of companies, regularly gets involved in essentially unique deals, and uses a lot of financial engineering – makes a virtue and a selling point of investor communication. In each case, you know what you're getting, which is the minimum starting point for deciding whether or not you should invest with them.

In short, if your manager can't tell you what they're doing and why they're doing it in a relatively easy to understand way, then chances are they lack conviction and discipline in their own process. And that means you don't want to invest with them, because ultimately that's the skill you are trying to find.

Having a defined strategy and clear communication also helps to offset the one big risk that a fund manager carries that you don't – career risk. By ensuring that investors understand that they will have good and bad years, and that they are investing for the long term, a good manager can manage client expectations and minimise some of the psychological pressure and practical problems caused by investors pulling their money out during hard times.

2. Concentrate! Find a manager with high conviction, low turnover, and no sign of index tracking

While active fund managers have a pretty poor track record of beating the market as a group, this isn't primarily down to a lack of stock-picking ability. A study by Randy Cohen, Christopher Polk and Bernhard Silli looked at the 'best ideas' of various active managers. They found that the stocks that active managers invested most heavily in did better than both the market and the rest of their portfolios. The researchers concluded that managers were incentivised by the structure of the industry to over-diversify – the balancing ballast in their portfolios was in fact largely holding them back.[12]

So you want to see conviction from a manager. By that I mean you want to invest with a manager who is going to spend time finding great ideas and then back them to the hilt. The portfolio

12 www.lse.ac.uk/Events/Events-Assets/PDF/2017/2017-LT01/20110224-Christopher-Polk-Best-Ideas.pdf

should ideally be relatively small (as few as 20 stocks is enough to diversify away the majority of individual equity risk, although it's not as cut and dried for portfolios of small companies) which means the manager will be putting decent sums into their top holdings. This also has the benefit that you can be fairly confident that a manager who runs a concentrated, focused portfolio is probably staying within their own circle of competence.

Nor, in most cases, do you want to see a lot of trading. Remember that patience is one of the sceptical investor's most powerful weapons. If the manager has a clear strategy, then they shouldn't need to chop and change their portfolio every five minutes – so you'd expect to see relatively low stock turnover. This metric measures how often the portfolio changes in a year – so a turnover rate of 100% would mean the entire portfolio had been sold and replaced once over during the year. There is no right or wrong level of turnover, but it's another useful measure to gauge whether the fund manager is actually doing what they say they will do. If your manager claims to be investing for the long term, but is in fact flipping their holdings every six months, you have to question whether they are entirely committed to their strategy.

3. Buy a small, boutique fund: an independent thinker

It's easier to beat the market with a small amount of money than it is with a large one. As Buffett has pointed out with regard to his own situation, the more money you have, the narrower your playing field becomes. When you have a small amount of capital, you can invest in tiny, neglected corners of the market where few others are paying attention. If you have billions, then you need to invest in stocks that can absorb big purchases without moving the share price. Those sorts of companies tend to be well-researched by your rivals, arguably leaving less opportunity for market-beating returns.

So why don't all fund managers stick to investing small pots of capital? It boils down to the difference between the art of investing and the business of being an investment manager. Michael Mauboussin sums it up nicely in his 2006 paper, 'Long-Term Investing in a Short-Term World'. "The investment profession is dedicated to delivering superior results for fund shareholders; practitioners tend to be long-term oriented, contrarian, and patient. The investment business is about gathering assets and generating fees for the investment company as opposed to the fund holders." In other words, for fund managers, it's more profitable to focus on getting bigger and attracting more money from more investors, than it is to focus on achieving good investment returns.

So, as Tim Price – investment author and manager of the VT Price Value Portfolio fund – puts it, investors need to seek out "asset managers, not asset gatherers". Not only do you want to find a fund with a manageable current level of assets under management, you ideally also want to find one with an explicit, well-explained limit on how large the fund will grow. This shows that the fund manager is not just a would-be asset gatherer, but a genuinely dedicated investor. That in turn suggests that you should favour small, investor-focused independent investment firms, rather than the big, profit-focused, fund management brands. The evidence backs this intuition up. More than ten years ago, Jack Bogle, the founder of Vanguard, took a look at more than 50 of the biggest investment firms in the US, and compared their investment performance between 1994 and 2003. Bogle found that not only did the privately owned firms beat the publicly listed ones, but also that those with fewer funds on offer did better than those with a wide range of funds. This makes sense – the availability of a wide range of funds suggests that a fund manager is keen to chase trends (launching dotcom funds at the height of the tech bubble, say, or China funds during the mid-2000s), which in turn points to an asset gatherer rather than an asset nurturer. This is one aspect of investment trusts which can be particularly appealing, as we'll discuss later in this chapter.

4. Skin in the game

If you are going to invest your hard-earned savings with a fund manager and put faith in their ability to grow those savings, then at the very least you should expect the manager to demonstrate confidence in their own abilities by putting a significant chunk of their own wealth at risk in their own fund. Some managers would argue that they have sufficient skin in the game simply by doing the job, but of course that's not what we're looking for as investors – what managers need to do to keep their job (avoid the bottom quartile and look convincing on marketing literature) and what they need to do to serve investors (deliver good returns consistently over the long run) are often very different things.

Put simply, managing other people's money is a very different proposition to managing your own. You don't want to be with a manager who sees themselves as a custodian of someone else's money – at the end of the day, there's only so much that anyone can care about what happens to other people's money. Instead, you want to be with a fund manager who has enough faith in their own abilities and strategy that they're willing to bet their own retirement portfolio on it. You want someone who is, in effect, managing their own money, and you just happen to be along for the ride.

This makes intuitive sense, but it's always good to have these things backed up by evidence, and in 2017, a working paper by Arpit Gupta and Kunal Sachdeva – 'Skin or Skim? Inside Investment and Hedge Fund Performance' – provided it. The researchers looked at a database of US hedge funds. What Gupta and Sachdeva noted was that a lot of these funds are primarily set up to manage "insider money" – in other words, family money, or perhaps a small employee-only hedge fund within a larger asset manager. For example, one of the most successful hedge fund groups in the world, Renaissance Technologies, runs a spectacularly successful fund called The Medallion Fund. As Bloomberg pointed out in 2016, the "fund almost never loses money" and between launch in 1988 and summer 2016, the fund would have turned $1,000 into a staggering $13.8m. But while Renaissance offers a number of funds that are open to outsiders, Medallion is for employees only – and it's also the best performing. And this, in essence, is what Gupta and Sachdeva found generally. "Funds with greater investment by insiders outperform funds with less 'skin in the game'", and they also outperform more consistently. This is in large part because the investors, as well as pursuing high-conviction strategies, make sure that the fund doesn't reach "capacity constraints" – in other words, as we noted in the point above, they don't aim to grow their assets under management to the point where it starts to impact on performance.

And in case you think that this is just for high rollers in hedge funds, similar results have been found for 'ordinary' funds in the US – for example, in a 2007 paper in the journal *Financial Economics*, researchers Ajay Khorana, Henri Servaes and Lei Wedge found that fund performance "is positively correlated to managerial ownership".[13] The more money the manager had invested in the fund, the better it did (fees also tended to be lower, and the funds tended to be smaller). Meanwhile, other studies have found that higher levels of manager ownership also correspond with lower portfolio turnover, another generally positive sign, as we noted above. In other words, it makes sense only to invest in funds where the manager is eating their own cooking alongside you.

5. Low costs and fair fee structures

Related to skin in the game is the cost structure of funds. Firstly, high costs will erode your returns. Even half a percentage point a year can make a huge difference when you compound it over time. Now, given that you're paying the active manager to deliver

13   faculty.london.edu/hservaes/jfe2007.pdf

better performance than the market over the long run, this may not concern you – you're looking for net returns after all, and as long as those beat the market, you're happy to pay for them. That's a reasonable point, but it has one obvious snag – you don't know if the manager is going to beat the market, and by the time you do, you've already paid their fees, whether they achieved the goal or not. Moreover, research by funds researcher Morningstar demonstrates over and over again that one of the best predictors of future performance for active funds is cost – cheaper funds do better and survive for longer than their more expensive counterparts.

Secondly, you don't just want low fees – you also want a fee structure that will encourage the manager to do their best for you. Again, this is the sort of area where a small fund manager will usually have the edge. The managers are typically owner-founders of the business, so they care about keeping costs low in general; they are frequently motivated by a sense that the investment industry generally charges its customers too much; and, perhaps more importantly, a fairer cost structure gives them a competitive edge over their much larger rivals. In an ideal world, a fund manager would take a reasonable salary, and then have a large proportion of their net worth invested in the fund alongside their clients. When clients do well, they do well – and that's as far as their incentive goes.

That's not how most funds work. However, one good example of a fair, investor-centric fee structure is Gary Channon's Aurora Investment Trust. The fund charges no basic management fee. Instead, there is a performance fee of one-third of any outperformance the trust achieves over the return on the FTSE All-Share, plus dividends. Managers are paid, not in cash, but with shares in the trust. And there is a three-year clawback period – so if the trust beats the market one year but then gives back the outperformance over the next two years, the managers will have to give back their fees. As Channon points out in the fund's prospectus, "for most managers of most funds [this fee structure] would result in little or no pay."

Unsurprisingly this particular fee structure is not at all typical. But that's the sort of conviction and alignment of interests that you want to see when you hand over your hard-earned money to someone else to take care of. So scrutinise fees, and pay particular attention to any performance fee element – what is the benchmark the fund has to beat? And is there a high-water mark (if the fund does brilliantly one year – resulting in a performance fee – then hugely underperforms during year two, but then in year three rallies back to where it was at the end of year one, you wouldn't want to have to pay the performance fee all over again)? Remember – the more of your savings you hand over to a manager, the harder it is to outperform.

6. Be patient, diversify and don't chase performance

There are added risks to building a portfolio of contrarian fund managers. As Howard Marks of Oaktree Capital points out, if a manager wants to "have a chance at the big money" – to really shoot the lights out – then he or she must "assemble a portfolio that's different from those held by most other investors." If you behave conventionally, you'll get conventional results.

The risk, of course, is that unconventional behaviour cuts both ways. Unconventional behaviour at a party can make you the life and the soul – or it can get you barred for life. Similarly, an unconventional approach to investing can mean you trounce your benchmark and the wider market – or it can mean you badly underperform. Clearly, you're looking for outperformance. But for that to happen, you have to give your portfolio time.

In a 2018 paper, Ben Inker of US fund manager GMO notes that in theory (based on various statistical assumptions), you could potentially have only a 20% success rate at picking successful contrarian managers and still manage to at least match the return on the market over time. The difficulty is making your choices and then sticking with them. You see, these high conviction managers – even the ones who are good picks – will definitely have periods of underperformance. That's inevitable. A 2011 study by Aaron Reynolds, cited by Inker, looked at 370 funds that had managed to beat their particular benchmarks over a ten-year period – so these were all in the relatively rare category of active funds that had been successful over the long term.

Yet during that ten-year period, nearly all of them had lagged their benchmark by at least 5% in at least one year, and one in four had underperformed by 15% or more in one year. More pertinently – because it would test the patience of any holder – over three consecutive years out of the ten, half had missed the benchmark by at least 3% a year, and a quarter had lost more than 5% a year relative to the benchmark. Every one of these funds had still outperformed over the ten-year period – but during that time there were moments when most investors would be driven to sell (or to avoid them, given their past history).

This point ties in well with another study (by Amit Goyal and Sunil Wahal, 'The Selection and Termination of Investment Management Firms by Plan Sponsors', *Journal of Finance*, August 2008), that shows how bad even institutional investors are at timing. The study's authors looked at buying and selling decisions made by more than 3,000 institutions between 1994 and 2003. They found that investors liked to buy after they had seen evidence of a fund beating the market for three years in a row. But almost immediately after they bought in, the outperformance – on average – slipped or faded altogether. The same went for selling decisions. Managers were typically dropped from the portfolio after two years of underperformance. After being fired, their performance promptly picked back up. It's another manifestation of the 'buy at the top, sell at the bottom' tendency that our psychological tics enforce.

The problem boils down to mean reversion once again. Every investor – you, me, Warren Buffett – has a preferred way of doing things. No individual strategy is the 'right' one, but each goes in and out of fashion. So, as we nodded to in chapter 13, even a skilled fund manager will find themselves out of step with the wider market sometimes – often for long periods. For example, since the financial crisis in particular, 'value' managers have struggled.

So, ideally, you not only want to find good managers, but you want to find them at a low ebb. If you can catch the best managers when they are cheap and loathed, and about to mean revert higher – rather than expensive and feted, and set to mean revert lower – then that will help you to hang on to them through the inevitable harder times in future. And again, remember that you're not doing this for clients, which is probably your biggest advantage over the institutions. You don't have to justify hanging on to an underperforming manager to anyone else.

So as long as you feel comfortable that the problem boils down to the manager's style being out of fashion, or a streak of bad luck that is being addressed, rather than a genuine lack of ability or a dangerous blind spot on the part of the manager (which is why you need to insist on transparency and clarity when choosing a fund in the first place), you can afford to be patient.

And because you can't be sure that you'll pick the right managers at the right time, you want to diversify – have a spread of funds and don't have them all backing the same strategy. That diversification will help you to ride out moments of volatility when one or other fund is having a bad time.

7. Investment trusts make a good starting point

Investment trusts are often a good hunting ground for funds that have the potential to outperform over the long run. Investment trusts are publicly listed companies that invest in other companies. In effect, they are just listed active funds. However, this structure gives them a number of advantages over their rivals.

Firstly, it helps to alleviate elements of career risk and short-termism. Investment trusts are 'closed-end' funds – they raise capital at the outset, and if investors then want to sell, they have to sell their shares to other investors on the stock market. Open-ended funds, on the other hand, are hostages to capital flows.

If an existing investor pulls their money out, and there is no cash in the portfolio to fund the redemption, then assets will have to be sold to raise money. That might not matter if you own a portfolio of FTSE 100-listed blue chips, but it can get tricky for funds that own anything less liquid. This is why all the commercial property open-ended funds in the UK had to temporarily suspend redemptions after the Brexit vote. You can't sell an office block in a hurry, particularly not if you want to get a half-decent price for it. Investment trusts are free of this problem, which in turn means that the managers can take a longer-term view and worry less about immediate liquidity when considering which investments to buy.

Secondly, investment trust managers are able to use a limited amount of leverage (borrowed money) to amplify their bets when they think that conditions are ripe. So a manager can borrow money to buy extra shares in his or her highest-conviction positions, for example. As we are looking for high-conviction, concentrated portfolios, this is a potential benefit, although clearly it cuts both ways if the manager gets the timing wrong.

Thirdly, historical data suggests that these advantages have helped trusts to do a better job of investing, on average beating both their benchmarks and their open-ended rivals. For example, in 2017, Lewis Aaron of research group Fund Consultants looked at London-listed investment trusts going back over ten years. He found that – even taking fees into account – the average trust beat its benchmark in nine out of ten sectors (the exception was the US large-cap sector, which is generally viewed to be one of the most 'efficient' – and hence hard to beat – markets in the world). Meanwhile, broker Winterflood Securities, which issues an annual report on the topic, regularly finds that investment trusts beat open-ended funds over the long run. That's not to say that this will always continue, but it does suggest that the structural advantages are meaningful.

Finally, the pricing of investment trusts can also flag up good buying opportunities. Because shares in investment trusts trade independently to the value of the underlying portfolio, they can trade at 'discounts' or 'premia' to the trust's net asset value (NAV). Logically, the share price should reflect the value of the underlying portfolio. However, discounts may emerge as a result of a lack of enthusiasm for the sector, concerns about the sustainability of future earnings, or a lack of faith in the manager. Thus, a period of underperformance can lead to discounts widening, which in turn can offer a good opportunity to buy (assuming you are happy with the trust's overall strategy). It's worth noting that discounts are a lot more common than premia, although it's also worth noting that discounts in general have narrowed in recent years. With that caveat in mind, if you have already decided to add a trust to your portfolio, look for discounts that are wider than average as potential points to invest.

8. Rebalance – put your portfolio on contrarian autopilot

Finally, one way to push yourself to invest more when a fund is near its nadir, and to take profits or reduce your contributions near the top, is to rebalance your portfolio every so often. Rebalancing is a strategy that can be applied to any portfolio, not just contrarian ones – but given the propensity for investors to buy funds after a period of beating the market, then sell when they've been underperforming, it may be a particularly useful discipline for anyone trying to build a contrarian funds portfolio.

There are really only two basic steps to rebalancing. Firstly, decide what percentage of your portfolio you want to allocate to each fund. Secondly, set some sort of threshold which will trigger a decision to buy or sell in order to return to this original allocation. So, for example, say you have ten funds and you allocate an equal amount of money to each. Over the course of time, some will do better than others, and so your asset allocation will shift. The more successful funds will come to represent a larger proportion of your portfolio, and the less successful ones will shrink.

Now, when you review your portfolio annually or semi-annually, it's important to look at the funds and decide whether they are sticking to the strategy that made you decide to invest in the first place. If not, you may need to fire the offending managers (whether they have underperformed or not). But this decision should be made separately from your decision to rebalance – rebalancing is about moving your portfolio back into balance, not whether or not you think a fund or asset still deserves a place in your portfolio.

So, having decided on a set of funds that you're happy to hang on to, the point of rebalancing is to take some profit on (or reduce your contributions to) the funds that have done well and so account for a large proportion of your portfolio, and increase your contributions to the ones that have done less well, and whose 'weight' in the portfolio is lagging behind your original allocation plan. In other words, you are almost automating the process of buying low and selling high.

You can rebalance in a number of ways – on a set date once a year, for example. However, I would argue for a threshold-dictated version of rebalancing – so you only act when a fund moves away from its target allocation by a certain amount. For example, say you had 10% of your money in each of ten funds. You might not worry about rebalancing until a fund had grown to represent 15% of the fund or shrunk to represent 5%. That means you aren't pruning your winners too quickly, nor are you overreacting to every dip and rally in the wider market. If you find that you are rebalancing much more than once a year, you're probably being overactive – and as we've been pointing out throughout this book, that's the last thing a sceptical investor wants to be.

Conclusion

I HOPE YOU'VE enjoyed this book and that it has helped you to clarify your thinking about your own investment process and to become a more sceptical investor. As a final action point, in the spirit of all good practical investment journalism – if you were to pull out just three key 'takeaways' from this book to pin to the wall above your computer, make it these three:

1. **Nothing lasts forever:** People think in straight lines, but life moves in cycles. When a trend continues for too long in one direction, the world has a habit of forcing it to revert to the mean. Both the timing and the precise nature of this reversion are unpredictable. But when asset prices become unreasonably expensive or cheap due to extrapolation, that spells opportunity for investors who can imagine a tomorrow that is different from today, and are patient enough to wait for it to arrive.

2. **Slow down:** When it comes to investing, deploy your brain, rather than trusting your gut. Every investment you make should have a considered, well-researched rationale behind it, whether you're a fundamental investor or a technical analyst.

3. **Look for the incentives:** On average, when faced with a decision, an individual – be they a central banker or your next door neighbour – will take the path of least resistance. The challenge for you, in trying to understand their behaviour, lies in figuring out what they consider the path of least resistance to be.

I write about all of the topics covered in this book regularly in *MoneyWeek* magazine, and in our daily email newsletter, *Money Morning*. You can subscribe to both at moneyweek.com, and I hope you will. You can also follow or contact me on Twitter at @John_Stepek – I'd welcome your feedback.

Acknowledgements

Thanks to the team at Harriman House, particularly Christopher Cudmore for presenting me with the opportunity to write this book, and Chris Parker for his editing skills.

Many people have given me a lot of valuable feedback during this process, but particular thanks go to David Stevenson, Alasdair McKinnon of The Scottish Investment Trust, Tim Price of Price Value Partners, Phil Oakley, and *MoneyWeek* colleague Matthew Partridge (author of the very enjoyable *Superinvestors*).

I've been lucky enough to work with a great team, past and present, for the entire time I've been at *MoneyWeek*. But in relation to this book specifically, particular thanks to Cris Sholto Heaton whose hard work enabled me to carve out the time to write it, and to Merryn Somerset Webb, who very kindly agreed to write the foreword and whose work inspired me even before I was lucky enough to start working with her at *MoneyWeek*.

Huge thanks to my wonderful wife Teresa, and to my wonderful daughters – not just for putting up with me, but for actively supporting me and giving me useful feedback during the whole period of writing this book, in which I was a distant presence swearing quietly yet viciously at a computer screen in various corners of the house.

And thanks to my mum and dad, who always encouraged me to do what I wanted to do. I've finally published that book…

Further Reading

This is a curated selection of the books that I've either referred to in *The Sceptical Investor*, or which helped a great deal in formulating my thinking during the writing process. I've split them roughly into three categories (though most of them span all three) – books with practical investment tips; books that take a higher-level view of markets and investment philosophy; and books on psychology.

Investment practicalities: how to invest

Deep Value Investing: Finding bargain shares with big potential (2nd edition, 2018), Jeroen Bos

Extremely practical book by a successful practitioner of modern 'deep value' investing, illustrated with lots of in-depth case studies.

The Art of Execution: How the world's best investors get it wrong and still make millions (2015), Lee Freeman-Shor

Short but punchy analysis and conclusions on how the world's best fund managers avoid common investment mistakes such as holding losers for too long and selling winners too early.

Investing Demystified: How to create the best investment portfolio whatever your risk level (2017), **Lars Kroijer**

If you'd rather not try to beat the market, Kroijer's book makes the case for low-cost, low-risk portfolios and shows you how to build the right one for you.

The Little Book of Behavioural Investing: How not to be your own worst enemy (2010), **James Montier**

Montier has written several books on value investing and behavioural finance, but if you want to keep it less technical, then this edition of the 'Little Books' series on investing is a good round-up. For more depth, track down his previous and current writings as a financial analyst at GMO, and before that, at Societe Generale.

Anatomy of the Bear: Lessons from Wall Street's four great bottoms (2nd edition, 2009), **Russell Napier**

An in-depth guide to the 20th century's best contrarian buying opportunities. Packed with data and firm conclusions on what makes a market genuinely cheap.

How to Pick Quality Shares: A three-step process for selecting profitable stocks (2017), **Phil Oakley**

A former City worker (and a former colleague at *MoneyWeek*), Oakley is one of the best company analysts out there. This book is reasonably technical, but Oakley's logical thought processes and clear writing make it suitable for beginners – and if you are serious about stock-picking this is the sort of analysis you need to get comfortable with.

Investing Through the Looking Glass: A rational guide to irrational financial markets (2016), Tim Price

Asset manager and value investor Price takes a deeply sceptical (perhaps even cynical) look at the mess that the financial industry, central bankers, mainstream economists, and politicians have conspired to make of our monetary system. But it's not just a polemic. Price gives practical tips on how to design a portfolio that can thrive and survive in our strange era of near-zero interest rates and money printing – and beyond.

Free Capital: How 12 private investors made millions in the stock market (2011), Guy Thomas

Very enjoyable in-depth interviews with 12 highly successful private investors, all of whom deploy very different strategies, which are discussed in detail. Inspiring.

Crowd Money: A practical guide to macro behavioural technical analysis (2013), Eoin Treacy

Treacy is probably the best technical analyst out there in terms of putting charting into a context that makes sense to individuals who are not technical analysts themselves. *Crowd Money* puts charting into a behavioural framework, and is packed with real-life examples.

Investment philosophy: how markets work

Devil Take the Hindmost: A history of financial speculation (1998), **Edward Chancellor**

There are several chronicles of historic booms and busts out there: Chancellor's is one of the best. His in-depth descriptions of booms ranging from the South Sea Bubble to Japan's stratospheric rise (and fall) contain a wealth of detail, and also make it clear that while human nature doesn't change, the cyclical messes that we get ourselves into all contain their own unique features that make predicting the timing of any bust exceptionally difficult.

Principles: Life and work (2017), **Ray Dalio**

The founder of hedge fund giant Bridgewater is clearly thinking about his legacy in this book, which is part biography, part financial history, and part management bible. But his strong track record speaks for itself and it's interesting to hear about how his learning experiences informed his investment techniques, and how the market has evolved over time.

Templeton's Way with Money: Strategies and philosophy of a legendary investor (2012), **Jonathan Davis and Alasdair Nairn**

Enjoyable and detailed biography of famous contrarian, Sir John Templeton.

Contrarian Investment Strategies: The psychological edge (2007), David N. Dreman

If you're already persuaded of the case for contrarian investing, you don't need to read this, but Dreman makes his case with lots of useful data and a big dollop of criticism of the efficient market hypothesis.

Reminiscences of a Stock Operator: With new commentary and insights on the life and times of Jesse Livermore (2010), Edwin Lefèvre, Jon D. Markman and Paul Tudor Jones

The thinly fictionalised account of the career of Jesse Livermore, a US trader who made and lost fortunes in both the panic of 1907 and the great crash of 1929. In the end, Livermore's life is a cautionary tale – his trading compulsion arguably destroyed him – and it's a terrible shame that he couldn't follow his own advice. But this is a wonderful book, compellingly written and packed with timeless investment wisdom and powerful psychological insights. This edition, introduced by trader Paul Tudor Jones and annotated by John D. Markman, is worth shelling out for – it adds plenty of historical context and useful explanations of the more archaic terms.

You Say Tomayto: Contrarian investing in bitesize pieces (2012), Alastair Mundy

Witty, informative collection of client letters from one of Britain's best-known contrarian fund managers.

Keynes and the Market: How the world's greatest economist overturned conventional wisdom and made a fortune on the stock market (2008), **Justyn Walsh**

A picture of John Maynard Keynes the investor, rather than Keynes the great economist, and how he started out as a commodity speculator then evolved into a long-term value investor. Light on detail but an enjoyable, easy read that makes its main point well.

Investment psychology: how to be a better thinker

Thinking, Fast and Slow (2012), **Daniel Kahneman**

An in-depth discussion of our cognitive biases from one of the fathers of behavioural economics.

Think Twice: Harnessing the power of counterintuition (2012), **Michael J. Mauboussin**

One of three books (the others are *The Success Equation* and *More Than You Know: Finding financial wisdom in unconventional places*) by Mauboussin on decision making, behavioural biases, and investing. It's a good book, but keen investors really should seek out the wide range of research papers that Mauboussin has written throughout his long career as a financial strategist at both Credit Suisse and Legg Mason, covering subjects from contrarian investing to evaluating company moats. You can find most of them online.

Three Psychologies: Perspectives from Freud, Skinner, and Rogers (1999), **Robert Nye**

There is no investment advice in this collection of potted biographies of three of the most important thinkers in psychology, but it packs a lot of useful information into a small, highly readable book.

The Worm at the Core: On the role of death in life (2015), **Sheldon Solomon, Jeff Greenberg and Tom Pyszczynski**

Again, this book is not about investment, but it's an interesting overview of terror management theory and the research that backs it up. As with many researchers, the authors probably stretch their thesis too far, but many of the examples are extremely compelling.

Superforecasting: The art and science of prediction (2016), **Phillip Tetlock and Dan Gardner**

An accessible guide to the fallibility of high-profile experts, with practical tips on how to be a better thinker. It's also worth looking at the associated Good Judgment Project if you are interested in honing your forecasting skills further.

Your Money and Your Brain: Become a smarter, more successful investor – the neuroscience way (2007), **Jason Zweig**

A detailed but accessible guide to our behavioural biases and the brain biology that underpins them.